Other Works by Darryl E Berry Jr

Next Density I (2015-2016)

Exo-Communications I (2016)

The Master: Y'shua the Christ (2016)

*Travel Far I [**Audiobook**] (2016-2017)*

Travel Far II (2017)

Pure Non-Dualism and A Course in Miracles (2017)

My Journey through Gracie Jiu-Jitsu: White to Blue (2018)

TRAVEL FAR I

Travel Far Series Volume I

DARRYL E BERRY JR

Accomplishment requires training...
Knowledge requires presence...
There is no sin; there is only Oneness...
There is no guilt; there is only innocence...
There is no fear; there is only love...
God is.

TRAVEL FAR

A BEGINNER'S GUIDE TO THE OUT-OF-BODY EXPERIENCE, INCLUDING FIRST-HAND ACCOUNTS AND COMPREHENSIVE THEORY AND METHODS

DARRYL E BERRY JR

Next Density Publishing™
Peewee Valley, KY

Travel Far
A Beginner's Guide to the Out-of-Body Experience, Including First-Hand
Accounts and Comprehensive Theory and Methods
Volume I
First Edition
By *Darryl E Berry Jr*

Next Density Publishing™
PO Box 783
Pewee Valley KY 40056
USA
www.nextdensity.com

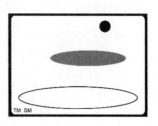

Next Density, including Next Density Publishing, Next Density
Publications, Next Density Center, and "Three Bodies Illustration," are all
trademarks and service marks under the exclusive use of NEXT DENSITY
RESEARCH EDUCATION AND DEVELOPMENT CENTER LLC.

Library of Congress Control Number: 2015904719

Trade Paperback:
ISBN-10 : 0996177906
ISBN-13 : 978-0-9961779-0-0

Digital:
ISBN-10 : 0996177914
ISBN-13 : 978-0-9961779-1-7

First Printing 2015

TABLE OF CONTENTS

ACKNOWLEDGEMENTS

To my parents – Darryl E Berry Sr and Janet Brealy, who sheltered me and cared for me during early fruitful and formative years of metaphysical and otherworldly research, development, and experience.

Elmer T Glover – my childhood karate teacher, who happened to also be a Voodoo priest! He introduced me to metaphysical studies – and study in general, igniting a passion of learning.

To all the extraterrestrial and interdimensional beings and influences that have helped me throughout the decades; taught me, guided me, and entertained me. These include Okanos, Bashar, Sasha, Germane, Anima, The Travelers, Orin, DaBen, Seth, the greys, the three beings of light, and the beings operating those nifty interstellar interdimensional spacecraft (*till we meet again*).

Louis H Ruiz – a great inspiration and teacher on the out-of-body experience. Thank you for all your teaching and shared experience. Much of what he shared with me is still ahead of my abilities and understanding! But I'm working on it.

To the great channels whose works and efforts have enriched me so, namely Helen Schucman, Lyssa Royal, Darryl Anka, Sanaya Roman, Duane Packer, Adrian Dvir, and Jane Roberts.

Robert A Monroe – whose writings, experiences, and efforts have inspired, entertained, and enthralled me. He is a pioneer in research on the projection of consciousness.

Joe H Slate – his meticulous and scientific investigation of auras and aura energy through collaborative research is inspirational.

Thanks to my 'brother from another mother' Michael "Patrick" Croudep for taking the photographs of me. He's always been there to support my efforts.

Thank you to all of the *AP/OBE Practical Research Study Phase Alpha* (2012) participants who learned and practiced my system of OBE techniques and methodologies and shared with me their progress, feedback, and observations. They helped me to once again validate the effectiveness of the techniques shared herein.

For inspiration, information, friendship, or all of the above, thanks also to: Elisabeth Haich, Samael Aun Weor, William W. Hewitt, Devin De St Germain, Bruce Moen, Kurt Leland, Robert Bruce, Muhammad Ali, Waldo Vieira, William Buhlman, Albert Taylor, Beelzebuub and the Mysticweb Group, Tom Campbell, Manuel Yousef, Sylvan Muldoon, Yram, Gary Renard, Richard A. Greene, Gavin and Yvonne Frost, Melita Denning and Osborne Phillips, and The Author.

INTRODUCTION

Do you remember going to sleep or waking from sleep and being unable to move as if paralyzed? This is commonly experienced at the start or end of an out-of-body experience (OBE or OOBE). Do you remember having dreams of flying or dreams of falling, accompanied by very real sensations of weightlessness or falling? You were likely unconsciously floating into the nonphysical while *dreaming* of flying, and then experiencing a rapid reintegration with the physical body similarly masked by dream imagery. Do you remember experiencing vibrations, loud engine-like sounds, gunshot-like bangs, or metallic-like clicks inside your head when going to sleep or upon awakening? These are also common occurrences during the initiation or conclusion of an OBE.

The out-of-body experience or astral travel is a mode of perception during which one experiences existing and traveling apart from the physical body. This is often experienced as an ethereal, energy-based body. You perceive and experience as validly as you do with the physical senses. Things perceived and experienced are as real as the book you are holding, or the screen you are viewing. You can fly, teleport, walk through walls, and travel extensively throughout space and time; and through various dimensions. Extraterrestrial (ET) life near and far, other planets, the far reaches of the Earth, other dimensions, the past and the future, other lifetimes, alternate timelines or parallel universes, the "afterlife" or "in-between lifetime" realms, and a variety of other interesting subjects can be directly explored and validated through the out-of-body experience. At the very least you can learn that you are more than a physical body.

Through OBEs you are able to observe physical events and validate your observations. Correlating experiences with other out-of-body explorers is also possible, as you can travel and experience the same things just as we could go to physical locations jointly or separately and confirm our experiences and observations afterwards. Unless you do something extremely strenuous while OBE – which is very difficult to do – you wake up from an OBE as refreshed as or even *more* refreshed than normal sleep, since the sleep state of the OBE is equivalent to a very restful and energizing deep sleep.

I share in this work several journals of my own out-of-body experiences, and a comprehensive system for learning to cause the out-of-body experience *yourself* so you too can experience this phenomenon. All techniques mentioned in my journals (and more) are taught in Part Two. This system is based upon my own recurring experiential first-hand investigations, my extensive literary research on the subject, as well as my experience with teaching others how to successfully out-of-body travel. I am sure you will enjoy reading of my travels. And if it is your hope to have the experience yourself, may your efforts be inspired! *If you apply the system I share herein you do succeed*, it's that simple. And as our individual interdimensional awareness expands we help to facilitate *not only* our own development, but the development and progress of the human race itself.

Darryl E Berry Jr
March 2015
www.darryleberryjr.com

PART ONE

FIRST-HAND ACCOUNTS

1 – MY EARLY EXPERIENCES

MY FIRST EXIT

My introduction to the out-of-body experience occurred quite spontaneously. I hadn't read anything on the subject, nor seen or heard anything about it. I simply experienced getting up from bed but leaving my physical body behind! One night, when I was 4 or 5 years old, I suddenly felt very heavy and lethargic, and went to lie down in bed. It was earlier than my bedtime, yet later than afternoon – around dusk. I was so lethargic by the time I got to my bed that I had to just plop myself down and pull the covers over me. After some time I started feeling better, and got up to tell my mother. But I found that my hand went *through* the doorknob as I tried to open my bedroom door. I looked back to see a lump on the bed under the sheets that I concluded was my physical body. I walked *through* the door and *through* the intervening walls into the kitchen, in an attempt to contact my mother. I tried to yell for help but no sound came from my mouth. I was able to observe her actions in the kitchen, and confirmed her actions later. A few years ago, wanting to confirm my memory of this incident, I asked my mother if she recalled this. She confirmed me as a kid running up to her, telling her of having been "out of my body."

FLOATING AND FALLING

Later I had what became a nightly experience for some time – out-of-body floating during sleep. The sensation of floating during sleep is very common, and I would experience this regularly. This sensation may be accompanied or followed by a popping, banging, clicking, or roaring sound, a sense of vibrating, an experience of paralysis, or a sensation of rapidly falling. Unbeknownst to most, *the sensation of floating is usually the perception of an out-of-body experience in progress.* One time I'd become semi-conscious during sleep due to a floating sensation. I became fully aware because of a repetitive whooshing sound. I experienced opening my perceptions to purview the source of the sound, only to find that my nose was *at* the ceiling of my bedroom. I looked to the side and saw that the blades of the ceiling fan were going *through* me – the source of the whooshing sound. I looked down and saw a lump on the bed that I concluded was my physical body. Intense shock ended the experience; I experienced a rapid falling back into my physical body, terminating with a series of physical shudders as I landed and reintegrated.[1]

I concluded that the sensations of floating while sleeping and dreaming were *actually* floating out of the body, and the sensations of falling while dreaming – usually accompanying a dream of falling from a great height – were *actually* falling back into the physical body. Nightly floating experiences continued in a variety of ways. Sometimes I'd simply hover at the ceiling for an indeterminate amount of time and then slowly float back down. There would almost always be a loud bang or metallic click in my head, either like a shotgun firing or like the snapping of the fingers – at both the start and end of the floating experience. Eventually I'd find the theory that the pineal gland in the center of the brain is a mechanism of the out-of-body experience, and that its activation in the process of dissociating from and reintegrating with the physical body causes the clicking or banging sound in the head. I don't know how true that is. I experienced the clicking or banging sound mostly during this early period, and contemporarily only after I haven't practiced

-----

[1] I'd later learn that this shuddering experience upon fast reentry is very common, and is called a *repercussion*.

for a long time – which could mean that whatever faculty involved in "the click" develops beyond the need to click, or that this sound is simply replaced by other signs of nonphysical excursion.

FLIGHT VISUALIZATION

In my infatuation with flying characters like Superman and Mighty Mouse I would dream of flying. I tried to re-create these flying dreams, being that they were so enjoyable. I intuited that to imagine flying as I went to sleep would allow me to re-create the experience, which I tried – sometimes so strenuously attempting to focus and not fall asleep that my brow would tense and be fatigued as I awoke in the morning! Eventually I began to succeed, and nightly I would fly through what appear to be nonphysical dimensions. The environments would often resemble physical world outdoor environments or endless cloud-filled sky. This visualization practice, however long I kept it up, no doubt contributed to the ongoing and *seemingly* spontaneous out-of-body experiences that would follow in the months and years to come.

GETTING UP TO USE THE RESTROOM

I would focus very intently before sleep to have myself get up from sleep to use the restroom when needed.[2] Several times I'd successfully feel the need to urinate while sleeping, get up and use the restroom, and then go back to sleep. But I'd notice discrepancies during my journey to the bathroom – a chair would be where it wasn't physically, or the light switch

---

[2] This practice reminds me of a technique shared by Sylvan Muldoon, where one sits a glass of water out on the table and goes to bed thirsty and building up desire for the water. This is to motivate oneself to try to get water during an OBE and be alerted to conscious awareness. I've successfully used this "thirst technique," as will be shared further on.

in the bathroom or the toilet itself wouldn't work. Or I'd reach the bathroom and urinate yet still feel the need to urinate. And then I'd wake in the morning and find that I had wet myself in bed. I later realized I was actually getting up and going to the restroom in a nonphysical state.

MY 'TERROR OF THE THRESHOLD'

Another prominent recurrence was various beings visiting me during sleep. The most frightening of these was a being in the guise of the television and movie monster Freddy Krueger. Though I was terrified of this character I was fascinated with him, and would watch him on television regularly; and soon would have nightmares about him. He would chase me at night, usually around my neighborhood, in environments that seemed at times to match the physical world and at other times to be a mixture of the physical environment and nonphysical environments. Eventually I got so tired of him chasing me that I fought back. I eventually learned that these experiences were in some sense *real* – meaning as valid as our everyday physical experiences. And I began to see that this "Freddy" was an actual being – albeit a very sadistic one. But he was at least as real and sentient as the beings I meet while physically walking about in the physical world.

Over time I learned that I could control these experiences and environments, which is how I dispatched of Freddy. He was chasing me along the levy at the end of my street. I imagined waves and waves of children running at him from all directions, beating him fiercely. He tried to run but could not, and I stood back and observed the beating. That was the last time he chased me! This lesson would help me in future encounters with negative nonphysical entities.

BIG BEN

The more I had out-of-body experiences the more they proved to be valid experiences rather than just "dreams." I considered speaking with others about them but I resolved that since no one was speaking about it that these experiences must be commonplace and not worth mentioning. I wondered where others flew at night, and what they did with their nightly travels. I began to think of ways to practically use the experience, for instance to visit distant places I'd like to see. I decided to visit the Big Ben clock I learned about from my grade school teacher. At night instead of focusing on flying I focused on being at Big Ben. I lost awareness and became aware standing directly in front of Big Ben, with people milling back and forth. It didn't occur to me that since Big Ben is on the other side of the planet it would be daytime there. I was quite surprised and exceedingly buoyant that I succeeded. But I cringed as I became aware that I was standing there stark naked!

Without reservation I believed that everyone could see me. I started to frantically cover with my hands. It would have been comical to see I'm sure – I'd cover the front of me with both hands and then realize that my rear was showing. Then I'd cover my rear with both hands and realize my front was showing. With some music in the background it might have looked like I was dancing, as I repeated this short series of gestures. I saw no indication that anyone noticed me, but in the frantic nature of it all I didn't really consider this. After some time I was suddenly catapulted or suctioned back into my physical body, crashing into it with a rough series of shudders.

BEINGS OF LIGHT

Another recurrence was of three luminescent beings visiting me and telepathically or energetically transmitting information to me. I would sit up out-of-body and see three beings standing by my bed. They would stand to the side facing me – one stood directly facing me, the others to either side facing slightly inward, so that they made a semi-circle.[3] Then information would flow from them and directly into my psyche as if a great river of knowledge was being poured directly into my consciousness. One morning after I awoke I considered what I could have learned and found they transmitted packets of information that I could unravel, review, and contemplate.[4] I opened a packet that contained concepts I'd later read about in the teachings of beings such as Seth, channeled by Jane Roberts, and Bashar, channeled by Darryl Anka. While contemplating this packet of information I knew that reality is what we make it. I looked at the wall, and then was able to see *through* the wall. I focused on the tree in our front yard and I realized that if we believed or decided that trees grew upside down to the way they do now, they would. The world took on a grainy quality in my perception, as if looking at a faulty digital illusion. It reminds me of *The Matrix* movie series, how the digital world looks through Neo's eyes; more like units or fields of data rather than discrete objects.

For a time this visitation occurred nightly, but the experience was so intense that at times I would wake up sleepier than before sleep! I mentally yelled at them to stop, so that I could get some rest. The visits stopped for a while, and

---

[3] I would later see a direct reference to this experience of three visiting beings standing in a semi-circle by researcher Dr. Karla Turner.

[4] Robert Monroe called these nonphysical packets of information *rote*. Darryl Anka experiences this as well through telepathic communication with the Essassani extraterrestrial race.

then picked up at a more measured pace. I don't know for how long these visitations continued, but I suppose until I learned all I needed to from them. Other than that one time I consciously unraveled a packet I left the information in my mind, and I believe it has unconsciously guided me. It is of note that given other experiences I had around this time, and research I've done since then, it's possible that rather than being nonphysical entities these were physical extraterrestrial beings.[5]

PORTAL AND CHAKRA LINE

I became aware in a nonphysical dimension, a city-like environment, facing a large and angry mob. They started chasing me with clubs and sticks and all manner of objects, intent to beat or kill me. It was a large, dark city, like loathsome renditions of the fictional Gotham City of the Batman DC comic book; or the city from the movie *Dark City*. I ran towards a bridge that seemed to be the way out of the city. The mob pursued. I ran onto the bridge and stood at its side, looking over the railing. A few inches under the surface of the water I saw my physical body lying in bed.

I looked back to see the mob fast approaching, and then back down to my physical body, and knew what I had to do. I jumped over the side of the bridge towards my body, passing through a portal to my awaiting body on the bed. As I dove towards the portal I could see a multi-colored line of lights on the centerline of my body, which I surmised were my primary chakras.[6] The portal I went through seemed like a manhole in the ceiling of my room. As I fell into my body I could see through the circular portal back into the dimension I'd just

---

[5] See Chapter 4.

[6] Chakras and energy working will be discussed in Chapter 8.

escaped. The portal faded from view as I reintegrated with my physical body.

THE GIRL AND THE MONSTER

I became semi-aware flying through a nonphysical dimension in formation with a group of nonphysical entities. I looked down and saw a beastly giant chasing a little girl, who was frantically running for her life. I flew towards them and imagined a bullwhip, and used it to grab and thrash the giant about. After I'd thoroughly beaten him, to the little child's delight, I imagined a giant pink seashell on which she sat, and I encased her in a yellow, translucent sphere of energy – it looked like a yellow pearl resting atop a pink shell, the girl sitting inside the pearl. I flew her home, tugging the shell along behind me by a thread of light. I brought her to her bed and body, and then went home to my own. I remember visiting her OBE several times, checking on her to make sure she was okay. She couldn't have been much younger than me – I imagine I was about 10 years old at the time and she was about 5 or 6. It's possible that I became to her what some adults would have called her "imaginary friend," or "guardian angel," and what others might call an *invisible helper*.

DEMON-OLOGY

I was suddenly aware of being pommeled with batons by two short grey or silver colored demon-looking beings. One would hit me over the head, bending me forward. The other would hit me to the face, straightening me up. The first would hit me across the stomach, bending me over again, and then the other would hit me elsewhere; pummeling me around like a tennis ball. Amid the ruckus what I call "fail-safe" kicked in – I was suddenly catapulted back into my body, landing with a *strong* repercussion, as if every muscle of my physical body convulsed as I reentered. I was upset at the situation of getting so thoroughly beaten. I closed my eyes, relaxed, and intended to return, imagining what I remembered of the scene.

It was dark there, as if a closed room, or perhaps an alley. There was a single light source, up and a bit back. I materialized before the two beings; they appeared to be chatting and were visibly surprised to see me. I immediately went to taking my revenge. I'd beat on one, punching and kicking, while the other ran. I'd then *snake* my arm out, stretching it to catch and grab the runner, pull him in, and start beating him as the first ran, and then grab the first back. I continued this process until satisfied, took a glance around the area a bit, and then phased back into my physical body.

THE DESERT WORLD

I was around 7 years old when I spent a week in The Desert World. I became aware in a world totally unlike the world we physically live in. The entire world was apparently a desert, with sand dunes visible beyond the meagre nearby manmade structures. I worked selling wares and pottery items on an outside table covered by canopy. When not working I lived in a small sand-colored dome, and had my own room to one side of the dome, though I don't remember any adults or parental figures. Initially I was surprised and taken aback at this place. It seemed like a dream I couldn't awaken from. But after a few days there I thought that *this* waking physical world was the dream. My waking physical life seemed like some crazy dream *so ludicrous* to have believed. Things we take for granted, including much of the technology we have, seemed so farfetched and fanciful from my newly acquired perspective of the desert world. There were no cars, and no airplanes there. There were no computers, and no phones. There was no electricity.

After about the seventh night of sleep in the desert world I woke up there, and then I woke up *again* here. I thought several days had gone by here as well and was frantic to find my parents and let them know I was OK. When I found them they seemed like nothing happened. School was in an hour. This all happened in one night! But it took several days of living here in this physical waking world to see the desert world as the "dream," and *this* world as "real."

Time, like space, is a relative construct, so experience of time in different dimensions don't have to correlate – just like how some extraterrestrial craft can be only 30 feet across on the outside, but 100 feet across in the inside. My experience in this desert world was as real to me as my experience here in *this* reality where you read this book, an observation that can be used to question the reality of experience *anywhere*. We accept our habitual experiences to be so valid, and the things we encounter regularly as so commonplace and normal. Yet even in this world there are subsections of society that house an entirely different reality, such as so-called Native American shamanic cultures, deep within so-called black government projects, ancient monasteries or mystery schools, mystical or metaphysically oriented groups, or even life inside of prisons[7]. The perception and experience of reality we take to be "real" is only one example of "reality," each version valid to those believing in that version.

FLOATING AND FUTURE SELF

I haphazardly and unconsciously floated through the ceiling and roof during a spontaneous OBE. I had vague sensation and memory of passing through the ceiling and roof but became fully conscious several stories above the house, floating continuously higher. I alternated my view between

---

[7] See Damian Echols' *Life After Death* and Assata Shakur's *Assata*.

the roof of the house and the expanse of outer space, with the certain and terrifying belief that I'd be lost in outer space forever! Suddenly, upwards and to the side, I saw *me*. A future OBE or spirit version of me was there hovering in the air, calmly watching. The calm and maturity and kindness and clarity from this future-self shook me out of my anxiety and fear, and I just silently watched him as he silently watched me. At some point I woke up in bed no worse for wear.

STREET WALKING

A recurring experience I had as a child was of walking down the street OBE. I'd become aware mid experience, simply walking down the block towards the corner, noticing a bluish-white monotone color to everything, and a ubiquitous fog or haze or mist. One time on the sidewalk about 1/3 of the way from the corner I saw two small troll- or Gremlin-looking beings, standing on either side of a tall structure. The structure may have been 8 to 12 feet tall, was oval in shape, and was checkered with tiny red and black squares that constantly alternated their colors from red to black and back again. The two beings looked at me, while I looked at them and the structure.

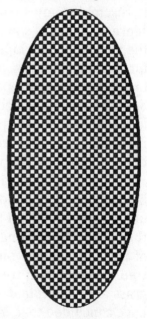

I soon recognized that the structure was some sort of portal. I looked with my inner vision *into* the portal and saw that it connected to a multitude of other portals through a series of tube-like conduits. My perception was that I could have gone into the portal and exited at any one of the other portals. But I was too afraid to go through, fearing I wouldn't be able to get back. I just looked curiously, and at some point woke up in bed.

PLACE-THERE SHIFT

I used to imagine or dream about a nonphysical location like the inside of a volcano, filled with giant mushrooms. I concluded that I'd be able to actually go there through the out-of-body state, and I decided to focus on going there rather than general flying. I succeeded, suddenly becoming aware standing in this locale, amazed at how closely it resembled my imaginings. It was like seeing a real life representation of something I'd only ever dreamt about. Over the years I've developed a few places to visualize and *shift* to for various reasons, mostly as an out-of-body experience technique or as a preparatory OBE practice.[8] One Place-There of mine was composed of several rings connected by several long hallways, all in a particular configuration. I equipped one room with a chalkboard to write on, to access to help me recall things in physical life, which I played around with only a bit.

As an interesting observation, after having it really built up and nice, I didn't visit my 'ring and hallway' area for quite a while. When I finally went back I found the objects of the place deteriorating. Several objects were an amalgamation of partially formed objects and inert energy. For instance a tree would be half tree and half colorless, bland energy. The grass and the ground were in parts fading into inert energy. I have concluded that when we imagine, the inert energy of the nonphysical dimensions are affected, and with continued imagination are shaped by our intent into what we imagine.

---

[8] This and any other techniques you read about in these journals will be taught in Part Two.

As we reimagine a locale the configuration is reinforced. We can travel to these areas we've made through imagination via OBE. But over time without consciousness reinforcing the imposed configuration reverts back to its original formless, inert state. I'd later discover that this inert energy is the same substance that composes *barrier zones* separating the various nonphysical areas.

MULTIPLE BODIED WE

One brief but enormous experience was to become conscious hovering in the out-of-body state near the ceiling on the opposite side of my bedroom as a point or field of consciousness. I (as point of consciousness) could see 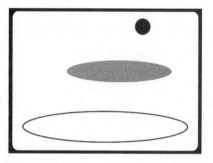 over my bed a nonphysical body floating near the ceiling. On the bed I could see my physical body. I concluded that we travel in (at least) three different forms: 1) integrated into the physical body, 2) as a nonphysical body, and 3) as a point or field of consciousness apart from both the physical and nonphysical bodies. It seems that the consciousness-nonphysical body combo can leave the physical body, and the point or field of consciousness can leave both the physical and nonphysical bodies.

This experience foreshadowed what I'd read years later of Robert Monroe's travels in *Far Journeys*; he describes detaching from his physical body with a nonphysical body, which he would leave hovering close to his physical body, as he then detached from his nonphysical body as a "curl" or point of consciousness, free of both bodies.

DANGER ROOM

At one point I used to battle nonphysical entities. It started with the Freddy entity, and soon after I started to *search for* negative nonphysical entities to battle. I became aware mid-OBE in a small cube-shaped room, filled with the most hideous of creatures. Some looked like demons; others like monsters with a large tail protruding from their waists instead of legs. I materialized for myself a large golden sword of light, which manifested as a hilt progressively materializing a blade, as if an invisible sheath was being removed. When my sword finished materializing the fun began.

2 – NONPHYSICAL MEET-UPS

MEETING FRIENDS

I've had several OBEs of meeting other out-of-body explorers, with various degrees of confirmation. The best so far is a meeting with my friend Louis, a highly practiced and skilled out-of-body explorer. I'd decided to visit him and to make it so I could validate the experience. *I didn't tell him I was planning to meet him.* And before going OBE I imagined myself in a long white robe, with a golden band around the chest/torso area of the robe. I went OBE and had a groggy experience of meeting and communicating with him in the nonphysical. The next day we talked on the phone as usual, and I didn't mention the experience *at all.* Louis volunteered that he saw me in the OBE state, that I was wearing a big white shirt with a gold ring around it, and that when we talked I seemed drunk.

Another time I had a semi-conscious experience of meeting a school flame of mine named Lugenia, and three of her friends. She and I hadn't spoken in years, and then I experienced meeting her OBE in a nonphysical dimension; along with a male she was apparently dating, and another female and a guy she was apparently with. Not being able to communicate properly with Lugenia due to the jealous interruptions of her beau I flew off exploring. I remember seeing off to the side a kaleidoscopic nonphysical realm, where a plateau of ground stretched into the air and folded into a swirling rainbow.

Later I called her and told her about this experience of seeing her, and she told me that she is almost always in the company of the same 3 people, that they go just about everywhere together: her boyfriend, her best female friend, and her best female friend's boyfriend. This experience was another confirmation that people habitually travel but are often unconscious of the experience in their waking life.

MEETING KEN

Another OBE meeting experience I had was with the *A Course in Miracles* teacher Kenneth Wapnick. I had a hazily remembered "dream" that I understood to be more than just a dream. I experienced a cafeteria that I'd regularly 'dream' myself into. This time I saw Ken there, but he looked conscious. He seemed to stand out from the dream. After the second occurrence like this I wrote him a letter, describing the experience. He replied with something like, "We should do it again sometime."

FALL, FRIEND, AND FLEE

One time I became semi-conscious on top of a building in a city that seemed like a nonphysical version of New Orleans, my old hometown. My spirit guide[9] alerted me that I was out-of-body, and I had a stark increase in lucidity and awareness. I jumped off of the building, still sort of unsure of my state but sure enough, falling dozens of stories and landing on the ground in a super hero stance with a loud thud.

I looked to the side to see what I could only describe as a *spider-truck* – a monster truck like the kind that drives over rows of cars, but with spider legs protruding from its sides as well as the normal super-sized wheels. Then I saw my high school buddy Melvin walking on the sidewalk. I tried to talk to

---

[9] I would later learn that this nonphysical entity is a deceased, tall variety of grey alien with two ridges on his head, who is called Okanos – my other-lifetime father from a grey alien lifetime.

him but he was in a dreamlike state, like *he* was drunk – similar to how I must have seemed to Louis that time. As much as I tried to alert him, and to make him aware that he was amid an OBE, he could not be made aware. Suddenly I was in my old elementary school, in a side section of the playground. I started playing around with energy, making energy forms and such, and then a crowd of people started trying to get to me. They were likely my own unconscious projections but I'm not sure. I made a barrier of energy, like a large, extremely thick spider's web, but the attackers started crawling through the large spacing in the webbing, and overwhelmed me. Suddenly I saw all black, and then all white, and then was back in my physical body.

ROPE PROJECTION AND WALT

At one time I used to regularly practice OBE in the living room of my mother's house. A mid-night change of scenery can help lucidity, and mindset. With a sheet to cover me and a pillow and blanket to lie down on I'd practice OBE on the living room floor. I relaxed, did some energy work,[10] and then started to alternate tactilely imagining climbing a rope and imagining myself to be in a different area of the room or in a different physical position. I allowed my actual physical body to remain stationary and relaxed. At one point I experimented with a notion I had, which proved quite effective. I physically turned to my side, and then tactilely imagined myself to still be lying on my back, and *then* applied the same techniques *from the imagined position of being prone on my back.* I started to experience slight vibrations throughout my body, which increased as I focused on the techniques. At one point the vibrations started to crescendo, and I focused on climbing the rope with all my focus and

---

[10] Energy working is covered in Chapter 8.

intention. The buzz and vibration increased as I climbed, and suddenly I experienced buzzing out of my physical body and floating forward into a standing position.

I walked towards the front door intending to exit the house, but was suddenly teleported to another locale and had various experiences. Later I was back in the living room, and I sensed my nephew Walter running in. I'd been telling him about the out-of-body experience, and we'd talked about meeting. And here he was, running up, as gleeful as ever. When I spoke with him the next day he didn't remember his side of the experience at all.

I decided to reintegrate with the physical body, walked to it and lay down intent to reintegrate. Nothing happened. I tried to *will* myself back in-body, or will simply to wake up, but still nothing happened. I surmised that my physical body was still deeply asleep, and I simply waited for it to awaken. At some point I lost awareness and awakened in the morning no worse for wear. Apparently when the physical body is in deep sleep, when most people would be nonphysically hovering close to the physical body unconsciously, travelers might not be able to reintegrate with the physical body. I have found that some physical need to awaken will circumvent this, waking us from sleep as normal if a physical issue occurs, for instance the baby crying. But if you just head back to your physical body and it's still in deep delta sleep you may need to wait a while to reenter.

3 – MEETING THE DECEASED

ROBERT MONROE

Twice I met Robert Monroe OBE – *after* he died. Fittingly I used his own Ident Method; focusing on all I knew of him as I went to sleep, with intent to go to him. I became semi-aware in a nonphysical area, in a class he was teaching in a nonphysical university. I actually disrupted the class, trying to court one of the female students. Still only semi-aware, I flew out of the window and saw one of my old high school classmates, whom we called 'Baby Girl.' She was sitting on a bench quietly studying a book, further confirming Monroe's finding that often people have active OBEs but don't remember them in their waking state. As I explored the surrounding area I saw a building across a large field, which I intuitively knew to be the *Akashic Records* building. It looked remarkably similar to a simple drawing made by Robert Bruce. Another time I saw Monroe in a nonphysical institute of sorts, and the facial image of a student of his, Bruce Moen, appeared in my field of perception. It seemed that Moen was there, or psychically aware of our interaction.

BENNIE BERRY

On one occasion I visited my deceased grandmother, Bennie Berry. She'd died about two weeks prior. As I went to sleep I built an *ident* of her; I focused on her, gathering everything I knew about her into my awareness, intent to go to her. I became aware in *the void* – a seemingly endless expanse of darkness. It's like outer space with no stars, a state I've commonly experienced in deep meditation. In the distance I heard her distinctive laugh, and looked in that direction to see an oval shaped cloud of multicolored light, with her face towards the top of the cloud. I explained to her what I knew of the afterlife, trying to help her along with her transition. She did not speak or say anything, but simply looked sweetly as I experienced her presence and communicated what I could. After a short time I phased back into my physical body.

4 – ENGAGING EXTRATERRESTRIALS

ET VISITATIONS

My earliest sightings and extraterrestrial encounters occurred when I was a young child, around four or five years old, before I knew about such things from television. I had several experiences of meeting or seeing extraterrestrials during OBEs and/or what could actually be surreal/dreamy physical states. I'd find myself standing in the center of the living room before the open front door of the house, and a classic looking short grey alien being would be standing just outside the doorway. It had a classic large, oval head – wider at the top, and large totally black eyes. We'd be standing there staring at each other. Other times I'd be standing on the front lawn and a spacecraft shaped like an outstretched human hand with fingers held together would be hovering right above me, just above our tree. Other times I'd be standing in the street in front of the house and *fleets* of ET craft would go across the sky. Frequent contactee Kim Carlsberg shared similar dreams in relation to her contact experiences, in her deftly illustrated book *Beyond My Wildest Dreams: Diary of a UFO Abductee.*[11]

As a small child I believed that these grey alien beings were my "real" family and parents, and that I was somehow and for some reason trapped on Earth in a human body, with a surrogate Earth family, and I longed to go back "home." In studying the experiences and research of Dr. Karla Turner I've learned that some extraterrestrial and/or interdimensional beings try to get their human contacts to believe this. It could

---

[11] Illustrated by Darryl Anka, contactee and channel for Bashar.

be to try to facilitate cooperation, and it could also be that the extraterrestrial is referring to a different lifetime. I also had the vague memory of being taught or knowing how to make an alien spacecraft, and would imagine getting the various parts and building a disc shaped metallic craft in the backyard that I would use to escape Earth.

Through subsequent research I wonder how many of these early experiences are actually hazily remembered or "screen memory" covered physical encounters with alien beings – including my earlier chronicled experience *Beings of Light*. Dr. Karla Turner, who found accounts of others perceiving visitations by light beings, found the beings to be physical extraterrestrial and/or interdimensional beings. Several times since I have seen physical extraterrestrial and/or interdimensional craft in the sky, and I have at least one vague memory in relation to these sightings of physically interacting with alien beings – including experiencing "missing time."

PHYSICAL WORLD ENCOUNTERS

A series of physical world sightings and encounters happened around the year 2000 when I was about 21 years old, mostly in New Orleans, Louisiana, in the United States. In the main one I saw flashes in the clouds and went to check it out and a craft came out of the clouds, apparently the cause of the flashes. I wrote an account on this experience in 2003, and reported it to UFO Evidence.[12]

This experience was at night, and I'm the only witness that I know of. The sighting was of a single object I estimate to be about one or two times the size of an average two-story house. The overall distance of the object away from me, including height in the air and distance away, I would estimate

---

[12] www.ufoevidence.org – on 2/26/2005 at 5:09:13 PM.

about two to four neighborhood blocks away after looking at a map.[13] It was about three stories in the air. The object was shaped like a short barrel – proportionately about half the size of a barrel, shaped something like five US nickel coins stacked atop each other. There was pink light coming from the bottom of the object, from what would seem to be a power source or propulsion system.

I actually initiated this encounter. I was motivated into this field of research by my childhood experiences and was quite infatuated with the subject for some time. Beginning in my late teens I'd read article after article, and read several books of first person accounts – including the classic *Fire in the Sky* by Travis Walton (made into a *very inaccurate* motion picture). I'd seen scores of sightings videos. I was preparing myself for an encounter, and now (I thought) I was ready and willing to willfully see crafts and beings, to initiate contact. I thought it would be quite nice to go away with them on their craft.

I concluded that most if not all of the aliens and extraterrestrials visiting Earth are telepathic. And being benign or benevolent, they would heed my telepathic call to see them. I began to spend time each day in meditation, perhaps 30 minutes each day, calling to them telepathically to see them and their spacecraft: "I want to see you. Show yourselves to me." And whenever I was outside and sometimes even while inside looking out the window, I had my eyes to the sky looking for ETVs (extraterrestrial vehicles). It took only about a month of daily meditative telepathic calling to have that experience.

I'd just gotten off of work at about 11 PM as usual, and was driving home, making my way over the high rise some 15

---

[13] I have a map illustration on my website at www.darryleberryjr.com.

miles from home. Looking into the distance I could see pink flashes in the clouds, and according to my research I knew that something was there. After all, lightening is blue. I determined that I would drive until I got to the disturbance in the sky, however far away it was. As I drove I realized that I was going as I would have had I been going straight home. I got off at my usual exist, still expecting to take some bizarre route through the woods or something to get there, and ended up going straight into my subdivision. The clouds were still flashing pink, off and on, and I continued to the disturbance.

The street I lived on is in New Orleans, Louisiana (USA), off of Willowbrook Drive, which itself is off of Michoud Boulevard. I drove down Willowbrook Drive and passed my street by about 5 blocks, and then parked my car near the disturbance; parking at the corner of Willowbrook Drive and St. Helena place (note that St. Helena place is a loop, and intersects Willowbrook drive twice. I was parked at the west intersection of Willowbrook Drive and St. Helena; the one closest to Michoud Boulevard). This is the same corner at which I used to play basketball as a kid. This area of the subdivision was less developed then, so there were almost no streetlights where I was. There were only about 10 houses in the immediate vicinity, including several houses on the left side of Willowbrook in front of the loop of St. Helena place; with much empty field around.

The light and cloud disturbance was over the woods on the other side of the levee. It was very close compared to most sightings I have researched. I turned off the engine, and watched and waited. The bottom of the cloud would flash pink like a strobe light, and then go off. Then it would flash again, and then off. The cloud continued blinking in this fashion, each successive blink coming faster than the previous. At this point I was becoming afraid. Given all my preparation I was *sure* that when I made contact I would run up to the craft and say to its occupants to take me for an interstellar joyride. But this was not the case. As I watched the cloud through my partially opened car window the cloud started blinking so fast that the blinks were linked together. Then the cloud stopped blinking, but steadily glowed, radiating a solid pink glow. As I looked upon the cloud, my window still partially rolled down and my eyes wide open, the aforementioned alien craft slowly and silently hovered down out of the cloud. A strong sense of fear came upon me, and I started winding up my window in a minor panic as though something might jump into the car to get me, or may already be in the car through the partially opened window! I was afraid to look into the back seat!

I wonder if this craft represented the same group of beings from my childhood experiences. Or perhaps this particular race frequents the area. Speaking to a local hobbyist fisherman he told me of a similar experience – and I was just talking in general about extraterrestrial life. He told me about how when he was fishing on Lake Pontchartrain (the nearest edge of which is only about 2 miles away from that neighborhood) an extremely large light appeared in the clouds sending a giant spotlight down onto the water. Whatever was in the cloud was *huge* he said, given the size of the light; and whatever it was made no sound. After a time the light went off and that was it. A fellow fisherman friend of his was there to see it as well.

There are several images floating around the Internet linked to various sightings from Gulf Breeze, Florida, that show a craft of a type – or artwork *deftly* approximating a craft type – which reflects very well the type of craft that I saw, and from the exact angle that I saw mine.[14] I think that the craft the

---

[14] This image is readily available online on several unconnected websites, and I received no response from website owners on its

fisherman was present to and the craft that I saw are of the same type, from the same race or civilization of beings.

Back to my sighting, I locked the car door, rolled the window up, fumbling as I did for I was sure not to take my eyes off of this craft. The bottom of the craft was hollowed in, as if under the stack of coins there was a shallow, downward facing bowl carved in. In this shallow downward facing bowl was a light like a moving pink neon sign, or a long and thick convoluted pink glowing strand of cable erratically moving about like an ornery snake. In the background of this moving neon sign-like line of moving light was a softer pink glow that filled the entire bottom crevice of the craft. I also remember seeing something like circular windows around the entire circumference of the craft, something like the little circular porthole windows one would see around a tug boat.

The craft seemed to stay out of the cloud for only a matter of seconds, as if the beings piloting it endeavored to answer my call of letting me see, and then go back about their business. Or perhaps my fear told them that that was enough. Though I didn't pay much attention to it at the time, the craft went back up a noticeable relative distance away from where it came out of the cloud. It seemed to enter back up into the cloud for instance slightly to the right from where it exited. And there was not a smooth transition between descent and subsequent ascent. It was like watching a movie and someone cut out everything that happened in the middle of a scene, in this case leaving only the craft coming out of the cloud and pasting that to its eventual reentry. Only the abrupt reentry and its slight but noticeable change in position indicated that

---

ownership, so I am assuming it is in the public domain. If not inform me and I'll remove this image from future printings of *Travel Far*. This one is from www.rense.com/general43/tm_nov.htm

a noticeable portion of the experience was missing. And something WAS missing – a sizable amount of time.

The entire episode according to my conscious memory at the time could not have taken more than 2 minutes from the time I parked my car to when the craft was reentering the cloud. I started my car, drove back home, and it was 1:00 AM! I know that it only took about 30 minutes to get home from work. I drove an extra 5 blocks or so down past my street, so it would have been 11:45 PM at the latest, by the time I got home. Yet when checking the time after I drove the half a mile back home, nearly an hour and a half had gone by! I was dazed and restless. I think I was experiencing minor shock. I remember stumbling as I walked through the hallway, and I have a faint memory of someone (or something) helping me to my bedroom. When I consider that missing time I am certain that I have had direct physical contact but have blocked the memory. At reaching my bed it seems that I plopped down and went to sleep.

It seems that this general period of time was filled with encounters. It appears that a certain group of ETs certainly took my invitation to heart. And I say a certain group of extraterrestrials because I saw manifestations of this same type of extraterrestrial craft on three other occasions. One night I had the urge to walk to the gas station a mile away, to get a snack of peanuts. It'd become almost a ritual that I happily performed several nights per week. I'd walk to the gas station, buy some shelled peanuts, and eat them on the walk home, looking to the night sky for craft the entire way. This night was a bit unusual in feel, though the trip to the store had no major changes in script. Yet on my way back home I saw a *massive* cloud to the North-Northeast, off into the distance towards Lake Pontchartrain – perhaps over the lake, I thought.

This massive cloud had a relatively small spherical area within it to the bottom-right that glowed in a kaleidoscope of colors. Red, green, blue, orange... it was like a spherical rainbow, the colors constantly shifting, and a large circular area around this phenomenon had a steady glow. I turned to see the source of a sound that approached in the air from behind me, and I perceived a black, unmarked helicopter flying low overhead, heading straight for the disturbance. It was flying low enough to clearly see the windows and frame of the helicopter, though the windows were far too tinted to make out any specifics of what was inside. I seemed to be able to see the rivets and bolts that kept the body of the craft together. As I walked home I looked at this disturbance in the cloud, and saw this black unmarked helicopter making its way straight for the disturbance. I continued home, not waiting to be the specific attention of either the disturbance in the cloud or the passengers of the helicopter.

Over the years I've reconsidered that helicopter. For it to be so low I did not feel any proof that it was there – or at least that it was in fact a helicopter. A helicopter that low overhead would've produced a maelstrom of wind and dust or debris. In reading a book called *Masquerade of Angels* by Karla Turner I've learned that encounters with extraterrestrials can bring with it the sound of a helicopter, though no helicopter is present. Sometimes one person would hear a helicopter and others would not. I wonder if that was actually an extraterrestrial craft moving directly over me, yet being so close catalyzing my unconscious fear, and I placed a screen memory over it. Perhaps it was something else, or perhaps I didn't feel the atmospheric disturbance of the helicopter because of the surreal nature of the experience.

In another experience, with what seemed to be the same type of craft that I saw near my home, I was driving home from work at night and I saw some flashes in the clouds in the distance. I decided to follow the disturbance until reaching it, and this time I had to pass the interstate exit to my subdivision, and as I did so I approached a multifaceted disturbance that was filling the clouds for miles around. I made it to the core of the disturbance which was in fact *over* Lake Pontchartrain, the section where Interstate 10 crosses the lake. About a dozen areas in the canopy of clouds were glowing pink, just like the way the cloud glowed from which the craft came out that night. On either side of the Interstate 10 there were pink areas glowing in the cloud, making the canopy of cloud over the lake a show of lights. Around a dozen or a score areas in the clouds had the pink light as if from the bottom of a craft, and it looked as if a giant pinkish spotlight was going upon the water from the clouds.

I wonder how it is that I didn't run into the causeway railing, for my eyes were unflinching, surveying the entire experience. I looked to the right to see one disturbance quite low compared to the others, looking to be only about 3 stories into the air. The light coming out of this cloud shown like a massive spotlight upon a structure or home that mimics a miniature castle, in a sort of theme park like area off the interstate, on the banks of Lake Pontchartrain. This area is on the east side of the lake, about a mile or two away from the causeway. The lighted area of cloud was right over the little building, right over it! I could see the cloud glowing. I could see how the spotlight-like glow was refracted by the moisture in the air, and I could see the light beaming down upon the ground and upon the structure. I could see the reflection of light off of the structure. I continued driving and looking until I was making it over the lake, in awe and wonder.

I remember seeing another car coming west on the other side of the causeway. I crossed the lake and made my way back, and I don't remember seeing the lights in the sky on the return trip. As a matter of fact at some point it seemed like a pinkish light was directly over my car and then suddenly all of the lights were gone and I was driving across the causeway;

then I turned around and came back on the other side of the causeway and headed home. The entire time I never looked at my watch or the car clock to see what time frames were involved.

Another experience I had with apparently the same type of craft was a year or so before, when driving home from Georgia about 800 miles (a 10 hour drive) from New Orleans. I used to frequently visit Georgia, and I would always be looking for alien craft. I would travel to Georgia during the day, and always come back at night, so that I was able to drive all night looking into the sky for extraterrestrial craft. I would sometimes park on the side of the interstate in areas of the drive where there were no lights, and spend time looking into the sky free from the ambient lights of the city. One night while driving home, far ahead of me at the horizon, I saw two large glowing clouds. I imagine I had to be in Georgia or Alabama at the time. The sky was covered with a canopy of could, as if it were the ceiling of the Earth, and these two large oval shaped clouds stood out as the only two formations of cloud separate from this canopy. I knew it was "UFO" activity, so I looked unflinchingly. These two large clouds obviously had something in them that was causing pink glows and flashes of light – both a steady stream of pink and flashes of brighter pink at intervals. The interstate where I was had a straightaway for miles and they were directly ahead of me.

After a while the glow and flashing picked up. The flashes intensified, and then a pink bolt of lightning came from one cloud to the other. Shortly after the pink bolt of energy went between clouds one of the lights took off, and the other took off as well. If my eyes weren't fixed on the event I could have missed it. To illustrate, wave your hand briskly past your eyes so that you see a streak behind your hands. That is what I saw. But instead of a hand it was two parallel streaks of bright pink light that went straight overhead, on either side of my car moving seemingly right above the canopy of cloud, or maybe even 'sliding' upon the canopy of cloud.

Apparently the crafts took off at a rapid pace, with no acceleration, from a full stop to instantly many hundreds of miles per hour at least. They were at the horizon before me, and they moved so fast that they reached the horizon behind me *before* the steak of light dissipated! To be sure that I am making myself clear: if you would look straight ahead and wave your entire arm across your visual field from your right to your left you will see a streak of your arm following for the entire distance. Perhaps before your arm reaches all the way to the left, the streak may have caught up to the middle of your body. In other words, the streak 'wears off' so to speak, and is like a trail following your arm, rather than just hanging in the air. Imagine moving your arm so fast that you move it from one horizon to the horizon on the entire other side, while the very start of the streak is still there! When the crafts reached the horizon behind me, the spots where they started were still glowing!! That is how fast they were moving! It resulted in two parallel lines of bright pink light stretching from horizon to horizon; with more light in the cloud where they started. After a second or two the light streak disappeared, and the two craft were no longer visibly detectable as it seemed they disappeared around the curvature of the planet. Amazing.

OKANOS

I had a longstanding friendship with a nonphysical extraterrestrial named *Okanos*; he told me that he was my father in a previous extraterrestrial lifetime; on a planet he called Auntaunria.[15] He looked like a classic grey alien, *except* he was very tall, perhaps 7 or 8 feet tall. Also he had two ridges

---

[15] Spelled here how it sounded to me – Okanos is pronounced O-Kay-Nōs and Auntaunria is pronounced On-*Tawn*-Ree-Yuh.

on the top his head, like big, elongated temples going from either side of his forehead back across the top sides of his skull. My interactions with him started when I took up the practice of channeling through automatic writing and automatic typing. I had several interesting experiences in that way, and eventually got good enough that I was able to make contact with him.

At first my channeling was a bunch of gibberish, and then became more coherent; then I made contact with a being calling itself 'The One.' Communication with this personage was much more coherent. Eventually I made contact with a distinct consciousness. At first, for the life of me, I couldn't remember his name. I would go into a deep altered state and communicate with him, and during our telempathic conversation ask his name. He would tell me and I would be *certain* that I would remember it, and be very clear during the altered state of what he had just told me. But when the channeling session ended and I came back to waking awareness I could not remember. It took practice for me to be able to remember it. I have found that when we initially begin accessing altered states there is still a divide or break in conscious continuity between our waking state and altered states. This is why so few people remember nightly dreams or their spontaneous astral travels. With continued practice we consciously enter and exit altered states, remembering everything experienced along the way, while there, and on the way back. We develop a *flexibility of consciousness* that allows for a broader range of conscious multidimensional operation. A bridge is made from our waking conscious awareness through to altered state awareness, so that our conscious awareness can enter deeper states of awareness and bring back the information and experiences. This will be discussed in Part Two.

Eventually I developed enough to remember his name, through continued altered state practice. I was able to bring more information back from altered states, and eventually it didn't require as deep an altered state to communicate with him – or perhaps since altered states were becoming more familiar the state did not *seem* as deep or altered. Eventually I developed the ability to talk with him in my mind in my waking state, as fluently as you and I could physically talk verbally. Sometimes I'd feel fluttering in various chakras as we communicated, especially when I was sitting down and relaxed; at first in the solar plexus chakra, over time the sensation moving up the chakra line, up to I think the throat chakra.

I eventually started to go out-of-body to meet him. At first my experiences of seeing him were largely through the hypnagogic images experienced in the altered states prior to OBEs. In the most prominent one he had on a hooded robe, purple in color, his face and hands shrouded in darkness. Gradually the robe revealed more of his appearance – the sleeves pulling back to show his hands, the hood pulling back to show his head. When finally fully revealed he had the appearance I described earlier, a very tall ridged-headed grey alien being, but as if made of many points of light, like a cloud of light in the shape of a tall grey. Once I met him on a nonphysical mountainside, and he told me about the planet Auntaunria. He explained that we destroyed ourselves in war. He showed me the planet, which looked like a burnt spherical cinder floating in space. I reflect on the fact that with the technology we have today, were it not for various extraterrestrial races that would prevent such a catastrophe, we would be capable of doing such a thing on this planet. Another time I went into the aforementioned Akashic Records building and saw Okanos. I'd later see a color illustration of the interior of the library in an OBE-related book I'd read some time after this experience, and the resemblance was uncanny. The illustration matched almost exactly what I'd perceived while there OBE.

There were several bookshelves in the Akashic Records building, filled with books. The books were hardbound in brown covers, stacked uniform on the shelves. Beside this book room there was an atrium with a glass ceiling, with a balcony off to the side of the atrium's second floor. I perceived Okanos up on the balcony, and he hovered down towards me, in his cloud of light form. We had a brief discussion and then the experience ended.

Okanos also saved my life on two occasions. One time I was riding my bicycle down the sidewalk and he yelled in my mind to "STOP!" I did so, and just as I did a large truck zoomed out from besides a building I was about to ride by. The building must have reflected the sound of the truck, and the truck was moving very fast. No doubt had I kept riding I would have been hit and run over. Another time I was riding my bike to work as usual and he advised me to take another route, a slightly longer route that ended up at the same location. At this point I was accustomed to following his guidance and I did so without question. When I pulled up in front of work I saw two young men hiding behind cars as if waiting for someone, one of them holding metal batons of some kind in his hands. They were looking in the direction I would normally come from, and from that direction they would have been hidden from me. But since I came from the opposite direction they were in plain view and looking away from me. One of them saw me and exclaimed, "He's coming from the other way!" I saw the work security guard notice the situation and start to walk away towards the building. I rode into my work parking lot, realizing had I come via my normal route I might have gotten jumped by those two guys.

ALIEN FACES

I went into a meditative state intent to meet or perceive extraterrestrials. I lost awareness, brought back to awareness by the perception of an alien-looking being staring at me, its face directly above and in front of mine. Physically I was on the floor, lying on my back on a blanket, and it was as if the being was standing or hovering over me, putting his face only inches before my own. I stared back for a while, with some shock that it worked, and some trepidation at his alien looking appearance. He had a humanoid face – forehead, two eyes, a nose, and a mouth. But the coloration of his skin was unlike any human's. His or its skin was brown, but a different type of brown. Its head was more oval shaped, like a mix between the shape of a classic grey's head and an Earth human's head. And its eyes were smaller than a human's eyes, as was its nose. Its mouth was smaller than an Earth human's mouth, but with less difference from Earth human features than the eyes and nose were. I soon decided to reintegrate with the physical body, and my perception of him faded away. The beings of the widely observed 2-mile wide boomerang-shaped extraterrestrial craft that hovered over and around the state of Arizona in the late 90s are identified by Bashar the extraterrestrial as a hybrid race he called the Yahyel or the Shalanaya. He said that this is the race that would make the first government-acknowledged contact with the human race. I intuit that this being is a member of that civilization.

Seeing alien faces is a regular occurrence for me. If I go into altered states with intent to see ETs I'll see alien-looking faces in my visual imagery, as if directly in front of my face – sometimes looking at me, and sometimes seemingly showing me profiles of their faces. I gather from Adrian Dvir[16] that ETs

---

[16] Author of *X3, Healing, Entities, and Aliens*

are regularly and frequently about, even during broad daylight. They have technologies that allow them to be invisible to radar and our visual perception, but by going into altered states they can be visually perceived and sensed.

5 – The Nonphysical

The Source and the Thiaooubans

A very prominent experience is that of meeting what I called *The Source*. I was in a very depressed state at the time, and wanted some kind of reassurance there was something more, or some kind of comfort from something *higher*. I had an idea of "The Source," some universal source of being. I wanted to meet It. I sought both "within and without" for The Source – I wasn't exactly sure where to find it. I got into a kneeling position, placed my overlapping hands onto the floor, and then my forehead to the back of the top hand. I *simultaneously* went into the depths of my being and into the far reaches of existence, searching for The Source. I intended, willed, and searched. Suddenly I was before a large spherical object that was *starry radiant*. But it actually radiated *shards* of itself that were as thick filaments of light, in all directions. The filaments remind me of thick pencils, except the source of the radiation as well as the filaments themselves were made of *pure love* and *pure acceptance*.

The waves of love and acceptance hit me, and I was awash with it. I became aware of my physical body again as I began physically to wipe tears from my eyes, while simultaneously being aware afloat before this radiant source of total love and total acceptance. Its constant waves of love and acceptance seemed to reach *into* my being. It started to lighten upon my self-consciousness, and the parts of myself that didn't like me. I tried to barricade my inner recesses to it, but that didn't work. It passed through every barrier and all my defenses, and yet all I found was pure love and total acceptance, even as it got to the core of me. Then it seemed to pass *through* me, and unneeded layers of my aura were seemingly blown off or carried away, as the constant radiation of love and acceptance moved through and past me – like how solar radiation blasts away parts of a comet. I went to The Source three days in succession, and the experience was very similar each time.

Immediately after meeting The Source I directed my attention to the Thiaooubans. They are purportedly a race of extremely highly advanced extraterrestrial beings that Michel Desmarquet met and was taken with on a journey to other planets, and to learn of other civilizations. They are supposed to represent the most advanced level of development in the universe. I had my doubts according to some things he related, such as that Y'shua (Jesus) was a member of their race that they planted here. Yet his book is still an interesting and informative read. I perceived myself going through outer space at *enormous* speeds, with stars moving past me like street lamps on the side of the road. I came to a stop after 10 or so seconds of travel, and could perceive a smaller source of love and acceptance in space, which I discerned to be a planet in the distance. I stayed at a very high orbit away from it. I perceived the planet as a much smaller sphere radiating love and acceptance, just as The Source.

Some of the revelations in Michel's book *Abduction to the 9th Planet* or *The Thiaoouba Prophecy* are quite at odds with some ways I know (or believe I know) reality to be. Thus I do question how valid is this planetary perception. When I did distance calculations according to how many stars I estimate I passed I came to about 225 light years of travel. I find that the Pleiadian system is about 444 light years away,[17] which could mean I simply found a planet of the same *quality* as the type I was seeking (advanced), though not the particular

---

[17] http://en.wikipedia.org/wiki/Pleiades

one he mentions, if it exists. At the speeds I was traveling a slight error in estimation – for instance of how many stars I passed, or the actual distance between the stars I passed, or how long I flew – could easily account for the discrepancy of a few hundred light years. Perhaps I'll go back, or attempt cross-validation with another OBE explorer or through other means.

I spoke with Albert Taylor briefly about such experiences as my Source visit – in his book *Soul Traveler* he speaks of a similar experience. After repeated visits he found his source entity to be his own higher self. Kurt Leland also shares a similar experience in his book *Otherwhere*. He was informed by a nonphysical entity that the source entity he perceived was the collective higher self of humanity.

ORIN

A very potent series of books have been written by Sanaya Roman and Duane Packer, channeling spirit entities called Orin and DaBen. There was a period of my life when I studied their books intently – and I still reference them regularly to this day. They help me greatly in many ways. I sought to meet with Orin and DaBen through the out-of-body experience, and did manage to see Orin. I didn't discern or perceive a definite form, but more like an "energy personality essence" to borrow the phraseology of Seth (channeled by Jane Roberts). We had a brief interaction in a wooded nonphysical area that looked like a field or park.

ASTRAL CORD EXPERIENCE, MAYBE

I've never come across what has been termed the *astral cord*, a supposed perceptible link between the nonphysical body and the physical body. But one time when I practiced my relax-move technique I had experience of what *could* be the base of the cord. I became aware in pre-OBE paralysis and relaxed and moved into an OBE. I rolled off of the bed onto the floor, feeling heavy like moving through molasses, and continued crawling towards the bedroom door. It felt like I was moving under water and that my strength was limited, so my greatest effort was still in slow motion. As I neared my dresser I felt a strong sense of protrusion or intrusion on the back of my nonphysical head, at the base of my nonphysical skull. It felt like something made of many strong cords or fibers was penetrating the base of my head, at the cerebellum region of my head. I could perceive or intuit a strong cable made of a multitude of interwoven steel-like cords or fibers. I have a strong visual image even now of what I sensed. I soon lost awareness, ending the experience.[18]

FIRE BEINGS

I reached a deep meditative state and perceived as if through a large portal or window into another dimension. Suddenly I was *in* that dimension, stuck in a position as if still sitting in the chair I was sitting in physically. My positioning was tilted forward, such that if the physical chair were actually tipped forward like that I would fall out of it. I was floating or moving down a street – *and also* looking upon the scene as if floating off to the side of my seated self. I was simultaneously maintaining two nonphysical perspectives. I saw two beings ahead of seated me on the road, made of fire, or made such that flames danced on them as part of their nature.

---

[18] Robert Bruce makes mention of an astral cord composed of a multitude of energetic fibers. An online acquaintance suggested that the anomaly was an alien implant, which I doubted.

TUBE ENTITY PROJECTION

I applied a technique of Sylvan Muldoon's by creating a sense of thirst and going to sleep, with intent to seek water in the dream and become lucid through the effort. I placed a large glass of water on the kitchen counter, after not drinking anything for a few hours. I glared at the water, thinking of how good it would taste, how thirst-quenching it would be, and then went to sleep. At some point I was drinking water from a water fountain on the side of a main street where I lived called Chef Menteur (also in New Orleans). I became consciously aware at noticing the odd location of the water fountain, and the fact that I was apparently there in the middle of the night! I teleported spontaneously to different areas, and ended up semi-lucid on Read Boulevard.

I saw a man skulking towards me, aware he intended to rob me. I was dreamy enough to see this as a threat, yet lucid enough to be aware that I could fly and get away. I let him get close to me, and then took off in flight, heading towards an interdimensional portal I perceived down a side street or alley off of Read Blvd. I saw someone in the way so I flew around this person, just as the would-be mugger shot at me. I shielded myself behind the person on the street, to my own surprise at such a selfish act, and then I flew through the portal into another dimension.

I saw a plane flying through the air, the kind with a single propeller and double set of wings. I dodged the bullet which made it through the portal, and took a swooping dive downward, seeing that I was high above an expanse of water. As I made that dive I could gut-wrenchingly *feel* the sensation of the direction change and dive. What looked like speedboats were skimming the water in a wide area, and an announcer seemed to be announcing a race. The boats skimmed around tall rock spires protruding from the water's surface.

Suddenly the "boats" started diving underwater, and I realized they can't be mere boats. I flew down underwater to see what was going on, and the immersion into water jolted me to full nonphysical lucidity. I could *feel* the coolness and resistance of the water, and suddenly realized I had limbs. Before this point, after entering this new realm, I was like a floating field of conscious awareness, my limbs being only faintly noticeable. Now I could feel my nonphysical humanoid form quite clearly, immersed in this cool, fluid, nonphysical ocean of water.

The "boats" were apparently some kind of creature or being, which looked like a large oblong organism composed of a conglomeration of tubes. If you would imagine a black ball of yarn, but instead of being round being shaped instead like a very tall, thin pear lying on its side; this is what they were shaped like. After observing the creatures or beings for some time one swam right beside me, much to my surprise. I could sense or perceive intelligence or conscious awareness in the being, as if it was observing me as much as I was observing it.

I became aware of a portal or teleportation mechanism towards the base of one of the rock spires. I went and nestled myself into the portal, and suddenly experienced myself back in the physical body.

ALIEN WRITING

I was living on Flood Street in New Orleans – Okanos was still robed and unidentified at the time. I used to practice altered states daily at this time, developing the "technique barrage" framework I often use to project. At this time I was using deep relaxation and meditation, tactilely imagining myself as a point of awareness circling the room along the walls, and visualization of shapes and colors to hold my awareness intact.

I had an energetic experience like butterflies were swimming through my body. It was a very curious experience. I also experienced something like Novocain starting in my neck, and moving down through my arms, my torso, and down my legs. Wherever this cool flow of energy went became instantly paralyzed and numb. I broke out of it and relaxed, and repeatedly observed this paralyzing occurrence. I started to get very strong imagery, and I began to see a sort of parchment with strange alien-like writing on it. Soon I saw a being wearing a purple hooded robe at some distance away from me, his entire head and his hands covered by the robe. *He* was showing me the writing. I would eventually become very familiar with this being – the aforementioned *Okanos*.

I floated up out of body a few inches, and experienced myself hovering about 3 inches off of the bed, still interpenetrating the physical body. I experimented with this, floating up and feeling myself light and airy and fully conscious, and then floating down and reintegrating with the physical body, and experiencing the heaviness and numbness and sleepiness of the physical body. I floated up and tried to throw myself away from the physical body violently, trying to backflip out. I experienced myself spinning backwards in place as a point of consciousness, like a ball rolling quickly in the water that was my nonphysical body, which itself was hovering interpenetrating my physical body. But *I* as a point of consciousness didn't budge completely from either body. I lost awareness but in the morning I vaguely remembered nonphysically making it through the front door and walking across the lawn, looking back at the house.

BOX-BEING PROJECTION

I was focused on trying to project and suddenly became aware of being poked. I felt agitated that I was being disturbed in my practice, and at one point literally pushed at what was poking me as if to yell "leave me alone." Suddenly I realized I must have just pushed away with my nonphysical arm! I opened my nonphysical awareness to see that I was floating horizontally about three or four feet off of the ground in a nonphysical dimension. There were two or three beings milling about me, perhaps just curious, the most prominent of which made of boxes of various colors. Imagine a being with a torso, arms, legs, and head, but each limb made of 4 or 5 boxes tapering down to the smallest box at the conclusion of the limb, the torso comprised of 4 or 5 boxes as well. Each box was a different color, colors repeating in 2 or 3 boxes at the most.

A difficult lesson to learn is that during practice one can disengage from the physical body and not even realize it. The more one practices the faster and easier the transition into deeper states of consciousness, and thus into the out-of-body experience – even to the point of the transition being imperceptible.

MEET ME!!

There was a certain period during my practices where during altered states I would hear a multitude of voices. I'd reach a level similar to what Robert Monroe spoke of where he heard thought-noise. He spoke of a depth of altered state at the frequency of thought of humanity, "M-band" noise. It was like being in a room full of light conversation. A voice in particular started to stick out, a woman's voice asking me to meet her. I'd sometimes get vague images of how she looked. I began to telepathically communicate to her to help me get out of body. In response one time during deep trance when I seemed unable to move away from my physical body she flew upward through the bed and tried to catapult me out by ramming into me. She flew up into my nonphysical back, and my nonphysical torso stretched up to the ceiling. It was as if my nonphysical head and my nonphysical feet were stuck to their physical counterparts, but the rest of me bowed up like a tent. She rammed several times to no avail.

NIGHTTIME VISITOR

A bit after midnight I did a 4-2 and stillness meditation, and then an energy working session. I achieved an altered state with brief flashes of visual imagery. After getting up and engaging in a series of physical world activities I lay down again at 2:00 AM, relaxing and not anticipating or intending much OBE practice until later. The alarm was set for 5:30 AM, to wake up and practice then. At between 3:30 AM and 4 AM I became acutely aware of the inability to move, as well as that someone was in the room, near the bedroom door. I became quite agitated, wanting to get up to address this intruder, and tried desperately to move but was stuck steadfast. Then I had the thought that this must be the OBE paralysis, and that I could project first briefly before addressing the intruder. But then I realized the importance of addressing the intruder and just tried to move and get up. I struggled vainly, trying to pry myself up from the bed. Then I seemed able to move a bit, but still could not wake up completely. Eventually I was able to physically move and looked about to room. I noticed first off that the room I perceived when I was in paralysis was much bigger than the actual bedroom. The actual bedroom looked small by comparison. And there was no one in the room. It was a nonphysical dweller.

I fell or went back to sleep to a vivid dream, and at one point of the dream I could float. I felt a floating feeling which pulled me up from the floor, and I glided forward slowly, crashing into the floor after I bumped into a table. The crash was slow and painless, and I laughed it off with everyone, secretly priding the fact that I could fly; believing this was physical. I got up, still interested in my newfound ability to float and glide, laughing with others as I allowed myself to float up and put my hand down, doing a one-handed handstand supported mostly by my floating.

Someone I was living together with at the time who I taught to have an OBE also had an experience of someone in the room near the door. She was in paralysis as well when she saw him, and then relaxed-rolled into an OBE. If I remember right she still saw someone there during the full OBE state.

THE GUIDE PLANE

During a time of intense interaction with Okanos he told me of an area of the nonphysical called *the Guide Plane*. On this level were spirit guides to incarnate entities. I became aware in a space that was made of golden light. The ground surface and the beings there were all golden light. I asked how they came to know they were wanted as a guide. He said that on that level our intent is as physical as a physical object here, and they can clearly perceive the intent for a guide, or for assistance. My attention was drawn to a certain area of the ground surface that grew upward into a conical shape. This, I was told, was the intention for guidance or assistance. A guide walked over to the cone and touched it, and there was a brilliant flash. This individual had made connection with a guide.

MERKABA SHAPE

I reached a deep altered state and rolled out of the physical body. I crawled nonphysically towards a wall of my bedroom, intending to crawl through the wall and fall onto the stairs on the other side of the wall. While crawling I saw a three-dimensional shape in the air, in the shape of a merkaba

– two tetrahedrons inversely interpenetrating each other. It was not a solid shape but an outline, like energy straws glued together.

SOURCE SELF VISUALIZATION

Taken with the idea of a greater consciousness that we as individuals are a fragment of, I endeavored to explore this. I'd read about it in the works of Jane Roberts and Seth, called the *Source Self*; Robert Monroe called it the *I-There*. A source consciousness deposits fragments of itself into time-space as incarnate individual beings – each source consciousness depositing several aspects simultaneously throughout time-space. The individual self is just a part of this larger consciousness. Some call this source consciousness *the higher self* and define spiritual growth as learning to perceive from the multi-incarnational higher self's perspective, just as some define enlightenment as seeing from the universal or planetary higher self's perspective.

I went into a state of meditation and attempted to see through imagination, and became aware in a void-type area, with bluish-white octopus type entities floating about, which I recognized as source selves. They had a round central area, with tentacle-like protrusions extending from them, each protrusion ending in a physical incarnation. And these lower level source selves were also extensions of a greater source self, which were also each one of several extensions of an even greater source self. There were a number of tiers of higher selves, on up to the highest source self that is the one mind projecting all minds.

It's necessary to trust perceptions when exploring. In subsequent trips to this level of existence I perceived another detail of the source self's makeup, a circle of energy under its bulbous body. Thinking I was just imagining things I blew the perception off, but when I made a drawing of the source self and sent it to another explorer (the same one who drew the Akashic records room), he sent a drawing back adding this circle underneath – saying that I'd left it out of my drawing – calling it an "energy spread" that is under each source self.

CAT ATTACK

I lay down and started to do relax-move but was too lazy to move. I went to combining 'arm-up' and relaxation techniques, and eventually to just relaxing. I fell asleep to vivid dreams – this was a period of frequent practice and my dreams had been vivid. At one point I couldn't see but I *felt* the house cat named Emerald biting my fingers very hard. This alerted me to my altered state, but I thought the cat bite was physical. I considered that I was in a deep altered state but aware of (what I thought were) physical body sensations. I thought that I could initiate an OBE, but wanted to make sure my fingers were not damaged. I went to trying to get the cat to let go of my fingers, while moving as little as possible. I wrestled with this, all the while recognizing that I was in an altered state, and trying to maintain it. I realized I couldn't get the cat off my fingers in this state, and the pricks of its bite were hurting. I needed to wake up to get the cat off. I tried to wake up and for a while I couldn't. I fought through and awoke, darting up to address the cat – but there was no cat. It was all imagined, or could be a nonphysical experience with a nonphysical cat-like entity – perhaps even the actual cat in question during an animal OBE.

This is a good illustration of how our perceptions and cognitions can be inaccurate – I was certain the biting was physical, it seeming so logical, relevant, and accurate. And it's interesting how in deep altered states we may overlook apparent physical dangers, for instance considering continuing the altered state practice even though a cat may be nibbling my fingers, or even though a burglar might be in the room as in other experiences. I think this is because on some level we know there's really no physical danger, and that we are perceiving nonphysically.

SHORT EXPLORATIONS

During relaxation and meditation I had good imagery, or was lucid in a dream. I was aware that I could go OBE. I rolled out, and felt slight vibrations as I seemed to automatically angle up to a standing position. I was in the living room of my apartment, right outside my bedroom door. I thought of exploring past lives (I'd been reading *Many Lives, Many Masters*), but decided to practice nonphysical walking. I got as far as the middle of the living room and then was somewhere else. I was in a building or office. Several times I looked at my hands – they stretched lengthwise as I did so – and then soon I fell into a dream. I awoke thinking I needed to be more focused on my OBE task. Another night I awoke and couldn't get back to sleep, partly due to noisy neighbors. I decided to get up and play video games and practice again later. At 6 AM I lay for practice, with the alarm set to go off in 30 minutes. I got sleep-comfortable and relaxed, making sure to breathe – lately I'd focus on relaxing on the exhale, and exhale more than inhale. This time I just let myself breathe fully, and relaxed *around* breathing rather than insufficiently breathing.

I started getting light imagery. I relaxed and focused into it and got full screen imagery, like a full screen movie. I was eventually full-fledged *in* the imagery, like in a lucid dream. I felt quite amused and accomplished, and proceeded to OBE out of the imagery. I relaxed and moved, and felt the characteristic heaviness and sinking, and I visually perceived an environmental shift, yet felt that I was still trapped in imagery and attached to my physical body. I went with the situation since it seemed to *look* like my living room. I stood up and decided to fly outside. I turned my back to the sliding patio doors and pushed myself backwards as if pushing myself while in a swimming pool, intending that I'll actually go through the glass doors (and not to a different dimension as often happened when trying to go through doors). I made it outside. But "outside" was like the backyard of the house I lived in as a kid and not my current physical location! I lifted up and away into the air, and at this point I seemed to lose awareness.

ARM UP, BODY DROP

One time I practiced the 'arm-up' technique while relaxing deeply, and suddenly my forearm fell and hit the blanket. With no loss or decrease in awareness I realized that my physical body just fell asleep and fell off of me. I was lying there conscious and shocked at the unusual separation, and just lay there until I lost awareness.

6 – OTHER INTERESTING EXCURSIONS

CONCENTRATION TECHNIQUES

During one period I experimented with the concentration techniques of the Mysticweb group, which was very interesting. Their methodology of projecting seemed very different from what I was used to. I soon learned to understand the dynamics and incorporate these techniques. Their technique basically has to do with being relaxed while focusing on something until you reach the out-of-body state – usually when drowsy. The two favorite objects of concentration for them are the heartbeat and a mental mantra. One time I lay for OBE practice and relaxed and focused on the feel and sound of the beating of my heart. In various sessions I tried various ways to apply this technique. Sometimes I would count the beats, others I would simply focus on them allowing myself to drown in them. This time, while sitting on my favorite chair, I decided to count the beats from 1 to 100, at 100 restarting from 1. While counting I suddenly felt my nonphysical head move downwards towards my heart. It was as if my head bent down to kiss my chest, but then continued *sliding down* my chest so that my face was flat against my chest. And then my face started sliding down my abdomen pulling my neck and chest with it. The strangeness of the scenario shocked me out of the experience! When I reinitiated the heartbeat focus the same thing happened.

Once while focusing on a mental mantra my nonphysical head started to move of its own accord. I was aware of my nonphysical head rocking and turning side to side, as of moving to music.

IMMEDIATE PROJECTIONS

A few times I experimented with short-cut methods to OBEs, which I don't recommend. A sudden experience of extrusion from the body can be very jarring. My friend Louis instilled in me the idea that deeper altered states are the home of the OBE; himself a staunch reader of Monroe. Louis went to a sleep lab and got hooked up to monitors and went OBE, and the technicians told him that according to their readings he could put himself into a coma. He was in the delta brain wave state during each OBE – I remember years ago making a post on an online forum board sharing this, entitled *delta is OBE*.[19] I also wrote to The Monroe Institute, and Skip Atwater confirmed the same thing. He said that OBE happens in deep delta states, and that through OBEs you can go to all of the focus levels described by Monroe, from Focus 10 (mind-awake/body-asleep) onward.[20]

Delta is a state of slower brain waves, and thus less brain activity. Thus he reasoned, if one would silence the mind, suspend all thought and thinking, this could lessen brain activity and thus shift into delta and thus into an OBE. I tried this, and would experience sudden juts out of the body. I'd be lying there, and would blank my mind, and suddenly I'd fly out at an angle as if my entire bed was suddenly yanked into the air. It was quite jarring. Shock would throw me back into the body just as abruptly. I decided that a more progressive entry into deep altered states was better for me.

Another instance of immediate projection was intense use of focusing on the heart. Deciding to *really* focus, and reasoning that a tighter, more singular focus would cause a quicker extrusion like mind blanking, I lay in bed with no

---

[19] Brain wave states will be discussed in Part Two.
[20] Focus levels are described in the Glossary of Terms.

relaxation or preparation and simply focused on the feel and sound of my heartbeat with all my might. I focused irrespective of any tension I might generate due to the intensity of concentration, like my childhood flight visualization practices. Suddenly a nonphysical hand would jut up from bed or my entire nonphysical self would jut up into the air or to the side. The shock of the sudden movement would propel me right back into physical body awareness, but I'd be able to focus again and cause another rapid exit (and subsequent rapid reentry). It was very interesting, but due to rapid reentry because of shock not very practical for me.

TIME TRAVEL

I've had a few very pronounced time travel experiences. In one suddenly I was looking through someone's eyes – as if in their body but unable to direct their movements, nor to direct my own point of view. Wherever their eyes turned I could see. As the person moved around I observed the room and surroundings through their eyes like windows.[21] Then I noticed this person writing something onto little white strips, and sticking the strips onto small plastic bags. The person repeated this strange process over and over. Suddenly the person looked up, and started to frantically look around the room as if shocked or surprised. After some time of excited moving and looking around the person went back to dealing with the strips of paper and the plastic bags.

Years later I'd unexpectedly moved into a sort of commune, and would sell incense for a living. Going through my normal routine of writing the flavor of incense on little white stickers, and then sticking them onto the incense pack, I

---

[21] Louis spoke of a certain area of the nonphysical where sets of two circles floated around, and looking through them he found them to be to look through incarnate people's eyes.

suddenly became aware that this was the experience I perceived years earlier. It was *my own* eyes I saw through, and this was the exact time in which my past self was looking through my eyes. Then I remembered how I started frantically looking around, as observed through the OBE, and realized it was my present self, looking around at the room, connecting the dots of the experience. And before I knew it, I was looking around the room, confirming that this is in fact the room I saw in the experience, and this is why I was looking around the room like that. Then I realized I'd just completed the circle, and lived the experience my past-self viewed through future self's eyes. The past influenced the present/future, and the present/future influenced the past.

In another time travel experience I was obsessed with thoughts of the first time I *could have* had sex, but was too afraid or shy to do so at the time. I was a little kid, and a slightly older girl was trying to coax me to have sex with her, but instead I ran away and went outside to play. Deciding to use my OBE abilities to explore this matter, I decided to see what would have happened had I decided differently. I focused on and intended on experiencing or perceiving the alternate chain of events as it would have occurred, and was suddenly that little kid again. It's not like I was looking through my younger self's eyes. I *was* that younger self again. All thought or memory of practicing OBE was gone. All memory of subsequent life experiences was gone. I was literally a kid again, living at that time for the first time as far as I was aware.

The experience started about 5 minutes before the choice point. This time, when we went upstairs in my grandmother's house, instead of leaving I went ahead with the sex. Soon after the sexual experience, as I was on my way downstairs, I was suddenly immersed in all blackness, and then all whiteness, and then back in my current time body with my current time memories reinstated. Yet I retained full memory of my venture into that alternate timeline. Now for that incident I have two memories, one in which I had sex and one in which I did not.

My perception is that I entered (or *made*) an alternate universe, a different reality stream or timeline, and *lived* in that alternate timeline for that duration of time. After years of looking into the concept I have concluded that in any scenario where we are inconclusive, or think back in regret, there is an alternate universe where the other scenario is played out too. The other universe is just as real as the contemporary one – in fact, from that universe, *we're* the alternate universe. This experience also illustrates the nature of consciousness and memory in relation to the simultaneity of time, and the ultimate truth that all minds or individuals are one mind. Even though I had memory of over a decade or two of experience subsequent to the time period I traveled to, *when I took on the first-person perspective of the target time I had no memory of anything subsequent to that time.* My memory, thinking, and attitude were all appropriate to the childhood period and personality I had projected into, and my memory didn't return *until* I returned to contemporary time. Except for that one different choice I made the same choices I made the first time – where I looked, what I thought, and that first time *was* 'the first time,' with no recall of future sexual experiences from this timeline.

If we are in fact one mind appearing as many, and all time is happening simultaneously, it is a constructed situation that we are unaware of the rest of time. We *trick* ourselves into thinking we actually are the temporary identities we undertake. We think we are the people we see ourselves to be but we're not. Only by persistent denial and compartmentalization of the majority of our being do we perceive and experience ourselves to be an individual mind, with memory of the past but unawareness of the future.

LUNCH BREAK PROJECTIONS

Inspired by Louis I began to practice on my lunch break at work. At one time I worked at the packing facility of a popular coffee brand, and would practice in the locker room on the benches during lunch. It wasn't the most comfortable place, as the bench was metal and I was squished up against the lockers, but it was fun. One time I reached a deep state and suddenly floated up out of body several inches, hovering slightly out of coincidence with the physical body, still interpenetrating it. I felt in my nonphysical chest a *very* rapid beat like a heartbeat, seeming like how Robert Bruce describes the *thrum* of the heart chakra. I hovered down and reintegrated with the physical body and noticed the slow, normal beat of the physical heart. I relaxed and hovered up a few inches and observed the rapid "beating" of the heart chakra again. I floated in and out a several times, observing the differences in state, and then concluded my experiment.

Another time at a later job I took lunch break at my desk, folding my arms and laying my head on my arms. At some point I reached a deep altered state, and someone across the office started to staple. I not only heard the sound of stapling but I *felt* it as well. The sound was tangible, and reverberated through my nonphysical self. Each staple was like the loudest and most palpable sound ever, and I *cringed* each time, *praying* this person would stop stapling.

At some point I nonphysically looked up from the desk, and was able to nonphysically sit up from my physical torso at the waist and look around the room. Suddenly I was in a reclined position as if leaning my chair back, *zooming* down a tunnel made of streaks of light. It was like a tube made of tiny multicolored comets streaked around me – or I was zooming through it. Soon my lunch break ended, concluding the experience.

PART TWO

THEORY AND METHODS

7 – Basic Theory of Practice

Altered States

An *altered state* is a state of consciousness different from our full-waking, standard, physical world awareness. An altered state usually entails a slowing down of the brain wave frequencies; with conscious awareness held intact. A word I coined for the practice and process of consciously entering altered states is *state acquisition*. State acquisition usually includes the application of relaxation, mediation, visualization, and/or concentration techniques. At the deepest end of the altered state spectrum is the home of the out-of-body experience, the delta brain wave state. The biggest difference between normal sleep and an altered state is that *with altered states conscious awareness remains intact.*

One popular phrase for the altered state is "mind awake, body asleep." *A deep altered state combined with deep physical relaxation is the prime state for producing the out-of-body experience.* Thus first over the next three chapters I'll discuss altered states in detail, as well as relevant fundamental practices and exercises, and then we'll get into how to apply state acquisition to generate the out-of-body experience.

Progress at state acquisition (and thus out-of-body skill) usually requires *relaxed* determination. Dogged focus can work, as demonstrated with my use of intense concentration to initiate experiences, but the forced progression through the states can also be counterproductive to physical and psychological relaxation. I have found that a relaxed determination provides a more gradual and gentle entry into altered states, while allowing for a more relaxed general disposition. My most seamless and controlled entries into the out-of-body experience have been through progressively reaching a deep altered state and then initiating or intending movement into an out-of-body experience.

The consciousness spectrum that we experience has been divided into five basic strata, according to the frequency of brain waves we experience. Four are standard, and one is more eccentric:

Our normal waking state has been called *beta*, a slightly slower brain wave frequency is the lightly relaxed *alpha*, slower still is the deeply relaxed or deeply meditative *theta*, and deep sleep, very deep meditation, or the out-of-body experience is the very slow brain wave frequency of *delta*. I've also come across mention of a brain wave frequency state even faster than beta, called *gamma*. Some time ago I heard someone interviewed on gamma, a man who if I recall had some sort of brain anomaly that allowed his brain waves to operate at an accelerated frequency. His brain waves would just cycle faster for a time; I don't remember him having any special ability or perception with the experience. I've also found a research study where it was discovered that objectless meditation, meditation that doesn't have an object of focus but instead works on developing the essence of a state such as a state of non-directed universal compassion, causes gamma brain waves. [22] Since our focus is on the out-of-body experience we'll be dealing with practices to help facilitate the conscious entry into deep theta and ultimately delta.

Perceptions in altered states include perception of things not visible to the physical eye. When a person is wide awake and perceiving energy, auras, nonphysical entities, cloaked or dimensionally shifted extraterrestrial craft, and other-dimensional worlds, or performing psychic feats such as

---

[22] http://www.ncbi.nlm.nih.gov/pmc/articles/PMC526201/

telekinesis, then even while in the beta state they are *overlapping* into the other brain wave states. There is an intertwining of beta waking-state physical world data with altered-state data and abilities. Such skill is utilized in remove viewing, where practitioners use their inner vision or clairvoyance (theta) to see distant scenes, and draw or write down their perceptions and experiences *as* they are doing so (beta). At more advanced skill levels it's possible to overlap the waking state (beta) and the deep sleep state (delta) and be actively in the physical body state *and* the out-of-body state simultaneously, as demonstrated with my *Source* experience where I simultaneously nonphysically floated before The Source and physically wiped tears from my eyes.

The ability to enter and overlap waking and altered states is also behind the ability to consciously perceive, interact with, and recall interactions with physical extraterrestrials. Most visiting ETs operate at our brain wave levels of alpha and theta.[23] Being in their presence shifts us into these states. This is partly why ET contact and UFO sightings can often be dreamy or surreal. This explains "missing time" – being unable to consciously access altered states most people are unable to consciously remember experiences *had* in altered states. Recall my experience with forgetting Okanos' name when I came out of the altered state, until I developed enough *flexibility of consciousness* to remember the information in my beta waking state. As we become more and more active in altered states our base state of consciousness will also shift to the alpha or theta range.

Practicing altered states also spills over into the idea of bringing more of the unconscious mind into conscious awareness and use. These deeper states are a way to access what we call the unconscious, the reservoir of memories,

---

[23] See *Preparing for Contact* by Lyssa Royal.

perceptions, and abilities that are shelved into the depths of our psyches. This includes the idea of using "more" of the brain. We can learn to consciously maneuver altered states and accept more of our potential, consciously accessing more of our experiences, and utilizing more of our capabilities. To delve into metaphysical development is to reclassify more and more of this ignored reservoir as conscious, relevant, and useful.

Through the out-of-body experience and altered states, rather than relying solely upon physical world sources for information, we can learn more directly. "If the public only knows what they're told, then it's pretty hard for them to come to any conclusions other than what the powers that be want them to."[24] The out-of-body experience and altered states are a way to access information free of external filtering. I *know* there is life after death, and I *know* there is extraterrestrial life, for I have observed and experienced it directly. My karate teacher actually learned his entire karate system through "dreams." He was taught by a nonphysical entity. Several famous scientists and inventors, such as David Adair, and Stephen Hawking (according to David Adair), have learned formulas and ideas through "dreams."[25] I imagine there is no fact or information outside of our ability to acquire through altered states.

PROGRESSION MARKER LIST

During altered states several phenomena are experienced. Here is a general order of progression marked by

---

[24] *The Disappearance of the Universe*, 101

[25] David Adair is a genius aviation scientist and Stephen Hawking is a world renowned physicist. In an interview David shared that he learned through dreams, and shared that when he met Stephen, Stephen corroborated the same thing.

the *altered state phenomena* usually experienced (with physical eyes closed) in each state. You'll find the listed progression of phenomena very comprehensive. The markers are arranged on a progressive scale of twelve denominations, each brain wave state broken down into three subsections of *light, full,* and *deep.* Note that some phenomenon are in the transition between brain wave states, so for example phenomenon listed as *deep theta* may also be experienced in *light delta* and vice versa.

   Beta is physical wakefulness, and is the reverse of the other states as far as the designation of "depth" goes. If you're in *"deep" beta* you are wide awake and intently focused on physical reality. *Full beta* is to be generally wide awake and functioning in the here and now of the four dimensional physical world (height, width, depth, time), for instance being active in the physical world after a full night's sleep. In *"light" beta* one may be less focused but still primarily focused in the physical, for instance towards the end of a long day.

   Alpha is a state of light relaxation. It's a good state for thinking and contemplation. In *light alpha* monotone colored shapes of light (for me usually a pale yellow) can be seen. This can be in the form of a field of dots, amorphous shapes or globules, or as *full alpha* approaches various static or animated patterns. A common animated pattern for me is a pale-yellowish dot with pale-yellowish circles continuously radiating outward away from it.

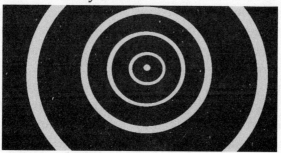

In *full alpha* you may also experience a quieter mind *or* an increased fluidity of thoughts and thinking. You may also experience automatic mind chatter. In *deep alpha* you may experience faint vibrations in the body – localized or full-body.

Theta is a state of meditation and reverie. In *light theta* you may experience multi-colored lights, shapes, forms, scenery, faces, or any type of multi-color visual imagery; usually in brief flashes and limited to part of the visual field. Any type of multi-colored visual phenomena, however brief or partial, signals theta *for the duration of the multi-colored visual, imagery*. You may enter alpha, see a flash of theta, and then go back into alpha.

In *full theta* you may experience various pronounced energetic sensations: tingling, prickling, and various other sensations. It can feel like prickly energy, static electricity, or as if insects are crawling across the skin, spider webs are strewn upon the skin, or as if water is flowing through or under the skin. Such sensations are due both to the increased flow of energy in altered states *and* the increased ability to perceive energy due to the altered state. Chakra energy centers, such as the third eye (the area between the eye brows) may tingle as well. Some energetic phenomenon can bring a sense of stark physical discomfort and perceived need to physically move – and it is fine to do so and then continue with your practice. With continued practice any discomfort will diminish or can more easily be ignored should you choose to ignore it. You will also experience more pronounced visual imagery, either in more detail or longer than a flash. It will cover more of your visual field or be full screen.

In *deep theta* you may experience very strong vibrations – localized or full-body, but strong; like rapid shaking, or as if holding an electric razor, or being jolted with an electric current. This may be accompanied by various noises or sounds: rumbling, bangs, clicks, wind roaring, crackling, or engine/turbine like sounds. Sounds may even cause tactile responses, for instance the bang of a gun-like sound may cause vibrations or shaking in unison with the sound. In *deep theta* you experience full screen multi-colored visual imagery, like watching a full screen movie. Focus must be maintained so that you are not lost in reverie which will result in falling into a normal unconscious dream state. You can also experience seeing or perceiving as if through the physical eyelids, into local or distant surroundings. You may also hear voices, environmental sounds, or various human/animal sounds; conversation and noises not related to the physical environment. In *deep theta* you may also experience rapid eye movement or REM sleep – it feels like your eyes are rapidly moving behind your eyelids. *Deep theta* is the edge of the out-of-body state; a sufficient state to relax and move or intend into an OBE.

Delta is the state of deep physical sleep, and home to the out-of-body experience. In *light delta* you may experience very pronounced tactile sensations – experiences of being poked, grabbed, pushed, prodded, or pulled. These won't be physical in nature, but nonphysical in origin, though they can *seem* quite physical. Making sure doors are locked, pets are secured, and so forth, can help eliminate mistaking such occurrences to be physical. In *full delta* you may experience numbness and heaviness of the physical body. You may also experience extremely strong and pronounced energetic sensations. This can vary widely, including sensations of roaming points or balls of energy. You may be vibrating so strongly that you wonder how you're being held together. In *full delta* you may also experience partial spontaneous nonphysical movement, for instance a nonphysical arm or leg floating off of the bed.

In *deep delta* you *are* in an OBE. In *deep delta* you may experience fully immersive imagery as if in a virtual reality movie. Focus must be maintained so that you don't fall into the immersive reverie which also amounts to being caught in a dream. You may try to move in the reverie but notice that your limbs are not working properly. This is because your physical body is asleep and your nonphysical limbs are still aligned with your physical body and can't move freely, and the movement in the reverie is just that, like a daydream.

A well-known *deep delta* experience is total paralysis; the absolute inability to move. This is a common occurrence when going into or waking up from sleep. The paralysis state is often accompanied by a related dream such as being held down or covered in some way. You may experience a feeling that something heavy is on your chest, or that your breathing is impeded – the nonphysical body doesn't need to breathe air. In *deep delta* you may also experience deep darkness/blackness or void, lucid dreaming (awareness amid a normal nocturnal dream), or various full-body nonphysical movements such as sinking, rising, spinning, or floating.

In *deep delta* you may suddenly become aware in the out-of-body experience state, removed near or far from your physical body, in physical-like or otherworldly dimensions. You may also clearly sense or perceive nonphysical or trans-dimensional entities in the vicinity, including nonphysical dwellers, other travelers, deceased relatives, extraterrestrials, interdimensionals, spirit guides, nonphysical shapes and objects, and nonphysical animals.

FLEXIBILITY OF CONSCIOUSNESS

Fundamental to achieving the out-of-body state is the ability to remain consciously aware during states that you have normally been unconscious in. Whereas before you would lose awareness and enter unconscious sleep you train to remain conscious during alpha, theta, and delta. As you practice regularly you'll find that you consistently progress more consciously through deeper altered states. For instance, at first you may experience almost nothing, or a few things from alpha, before losing awareness. As you continue to practice regularly you'll notice more and more things of deeper alpha, and then light theta. Then you'll consistently hit full theta, and so on. Simply keep practicing patiently and consistently as I'll outline in the Developmental Basics, Practical Considerations, and Practicing OBE chapters and you will progress.

As you practice, be aware of the depth of state at which you lose awareness. That point is your current *awareness threshold*, the depth to which you are able to keep your conscious awareness intact. The general goal is to consistently practice so that you move this threshold of awareness back further and further, until you can be aware at least through the deep theta state. From there you can initiate an OBE. Eventually, with continued practice, the awareness threshold pushes back far enough and sure that we remain fully conscious 24 hours a day. Your body may sleep, but your mind remains aware. Days and nights blend into a surreal, dreamlike, continuous reality. I reached this level during a period of frequent and regular practice during my early teens.

When I reached this point I wasn't ready for it, and discontinued practicing for a time so that a divide between waking and sleeping could reestablish itself. Recall my desert world experience in which I spent so much "time" in this otherworldly reality that when I got back to this reality, this reality seemed to be the dream. It reminds me of Bruce Moen, who began to frequently engage nonphysical realities to the point that he could no longer tell the difference between physical and nonphysical realities. He almost physically drove his beta world physical car (and body!) off of a cliff, thinking it was a dream. He could no longer tell if he was lucid dreaming or in the physical world.[26] Thus as you advance, if you develop to this point, be sure to be very conscious of which dimension you are in. Test your state by jumping up and down, not by jumping off of a cliff. I think with patient progress and open-mindedness to unfamiliar perspectives this waking world / sleeping world divide can be permanently abandoned by anyone.

See-sawing through the states throughout the day is very effective in developing flexibility of consciousness. The more dispersed are your movements through the states the easier it will be to move through the states. What I mean is, if your only dips into delta are during the night's sleep you may find it harder to remain aware during delta than if you dipped into delta a few times during the daytime as well. If throughout the day and night you regularly intersperse altered state practices with periods of wakefulness you can more easily move through the states in a conscious way and at will.

Flexibility of consciousness requires some degree of withdrawal from heavy investment in the four-dimensional physical world of beta. Each state acquisition practice and OBE session is effectively some degree of conscious withdrawal from the physical beta frequency of reality into other dimensions and frequencies of reality. I remember at times not wanting to sleep, being so anxious to not miss something in the physical world. As you can imagine during such periods of time I didn't experience much other-dimensional activity. My attention was too focused into the physical world. But at other times I was so anxious to go flying that I *couldn't wait* to sleep. I was home and ready for sleep early, mentally free of physical concerns or distractions, anxious to focus on engaging the nonphysical. As you can imagine my success rate

---

[26] *Voyages into the Unknown*, page 37

at accessing other-dimensional awareness was quite high during such times.

A beta-dominant reality focus is a tight, addictive focus that precludes awareness of other realities. The ideal is to *balance* the states, for example using our body's rhythms as cues. When wide awake engage the physical world. When drowsy or sleepy engage the nonphysical world. If you find yourself fighting sleep to stay active physically you're over-pushing beta focus and unbalancing yourself. If you find yourself fighting wakefulness to stay asleep or to practice more you're over pushing altered state focus and unbalancing yourself. A balanced, receptive approach is easy and natural. Ideally each brain wave state is to become as conscious and as natural as every other.

PARALLEL PROCESSING

We have discussed the ability to *overlap* different altered states. Thomas Campbell [27] calls this "parallel processing." Tom and several other participants of experiments with Robert Monroe experienced being able to fully engage the out-of-body experience while being able to simultaneously engage the physical – in their case physically dictating their out-of-body experiences into a microphone suspended over their physical mouths. Bruce Moen would be able to sit at a counter and drink coffee while also exploring nonphysical worlds. Robert Bruce experienced confronting himself during the OBE state, his nonphysical self entering the room while his physical self was still sitting in trance. I experienced being with The Source, bathing in its high frequency radiation, while simultaneously wiping tears from my physical eyes. Robert Monroe (in the nonphysical realms after his death) is reported by Bruce Moen as able to duplicate

---

[27] Author of *My Big TOE*.

himself and interact with several out-of-body explorers simultaneously. So with continued practice the flexibility and fluidity of consciousness continually expands.

8 – DEVELOPMENTAL BASICS

The following basic exercises not only help with the practice of OBE, but also with the general ability to function. The basics include *concentration, relaxation, meditation, visualization, mental projection, energy working, awareness,* and *psychic development.* It's not necessary to practice all of these. But the more of them you practice, and the more you practice them, the better and quicker will be your results in OBE skill development. I'd say the three most indispensable are concentration, relaxation, and meditation. The other basics are listed in a *sort of* suggested order of importance as well, but beyond the first three the order of importance is more personal preference. The first three can be described as required courses, while the others are electives which you can choose among according to your temperament and interests. I suggest at least two elective practices.

BASICS PRACTICING TIMING

I suggest practicing basics sometime *totally apart* from sleep and OBE practice. Any time of day or night will do. Being fully awake to drowsy is best; not sleepy. Practicing basics will help your ability to get a stronger and deeper progression through altered states by building and strengthening conscious awareness, the energy body, and clarity of mind. It's like doing stretches and calisthenics to warm, strengthen, and limber the physical body in preparation for physical activity. If you happen to go into altered states or OBE during basics practice, that's fine of course. But the intended idea for basic practice is to focus on the basic foundational skill. As a general rule, for every hour you spend practicing to have an out-of-body experience you should spend 1 or more hours practicing one or more of these basics. *If you feel that your efforts to initiate an OBE are not progressing spend more time practicing the basics.* Even with my years of practice and experience, when I've not practiced for an extended amount of time I require several weeks of consistent basics practice to get back my momentum.

OBE DAY

If you have limited time to devote to OBE development it's better to practice initiating an OBE only once per week while practicing basics daily, than it is to try to initiate an OBE daily and rarely practice the basics. Your actual OBE practice sessions will be less frustrated by failure in the process. A great way to do this is to pick one day per week to try to get OBE, a day when you can devote as much time as necessary, even the entire day, to the effort. This will make a more psychologically relaxed atmosphere. Throughout the week practice the basics, building up to that day when you practice to OBE. For a time I practiced like this and was able to generate an OBE each week on "OBE day," which for me was Saturday since I had the entire day. You can start basics practice now and practice them as you continue reading about how to initiate an OBE.

BASICS PREP

At the start of each basics practice session I suggest several deep breaths – full and deep inhales, followed by full and complete exhales – to help center yourself and set the tone for the practice. While breathing let all other concerns go and then put all attention onto the practice. In addition to the breathing you can tilt your head back on the inhale, and then tilt your head forward on the exhale. You can also breathe in through the nose, and out through the mouth.

CONCENTRATION

Concentration is the practice and state of being one-pointed in attention. It means to direct all of one's attention to one object or thought for an extended period of time. Without sufficient ability to concentrate you won't be able to focus on any technique or effort long enough and soundly enough for it to make a difference, which is why the Concentration basic is listed first. If you find yourself inattentive or falling asleep a lot during practice, in addition to getting more rest, try practicing more concentration. At the least I suggest practicing concentration twice a day – once in the morning or daytime and once in the evening or nighttime; before being sleepy. With any concentration exercise *don't try to push extraneous thoughts away. Simply go back to the practice.* It's about concentrating on what you want to focus on, *not* about pushing away what you don't want to focus on. You may need to build up your ability to concentrate – if there's strain rather than straining for a full five minutes of practice start with 1 or 2 minutes and build up.

Visualization-Concentration: Probably the best concentration exercise for OBE development is to practice visualizing an object from memory. In this way you practice visualization and concentration at the same time. If you don't practice visualization separately I definitely suggest this concentration exercise. Procure a simple object – for instance a pencil or ink pen – and study the object closely. And then after spending a few minutes studying the object, close your eyes and attempt to visualize the object perfectly. *Put the object down* so you're not simply using touch to help your memory. If you have forgotten or missed any details study the object again, and visualize again. A good session of this is 5 minutes total. Practice with the same object for 5 minutes, increasingly perfecting your memory and visualization of the object.

Second Hand Stare. Another great concentration exercise is the *second hand stare;* which is to stare at the second hand of a timepiece for a minute, placing the attention solely on the second hand as it moves around the dial, and simply bringing the attention back to the second hand in response to any wavering of attention. The numbers of a digital clock can work as well, either by focusing on the digital seconds counting by or by staring at the minute digit until it changes. Practice five repetitions of 1-minute stares for a good practice session. The first time you may want to see how long it takes for you to lose awareness, so you have a baseline from which to work. Don't be surprised if you can only focus 10 seconds or less before trailing off in thought.

Century Breath Count. A challenging concentration exercise is to sit or lay down comfortably and relax while you count your breaths from 1 to 100. If you hit 100 without a break in focus then you've finished the exercise for the session. And this exercise presents a situation quite similar to the concentration you'll be using during OBE practice, in that it is relaxed yet requires focus and attention. If you lose awareness or count, or forget that you're doing the exercise, start again from 1 and focus more on the breath and the numbers. If you seem tense, have a more relaxed focus – but the priority is still on the focus and not the relaxation. Focus on counting the breaths, not on changing the pace or depth of your breathing. You can place a hand on the chest and the other on the abdomen to help you focus. Start with 5 minutes of practice by alarm, and work up from there until you can hit 100.

RELAXATION

Relaxation is fundamental. With enough concentration to not lose awareness, deep relaxation alone can be used to initiate an OBE. While one can enter deep altered states and still be active physically I have found that progress is much smoother, and much surer, and much more comfortable, by progressing first from a physically relaxed foundation. *Naturally* parallel processing will manifest. Relaxation is not only physical but also psychological. One can't relax physically with psychological tension, worry, and mind chatter. This also is why concentration is paramount, and the deep breathing preparation is helpful. 30-minutes total of daily relaxation practice is sufficient. As a supplement you can practice relaxing as you go about your daily activities. You may be surprised to find how tense you normally are!

Basic Relaxation. Get into a comfortable position or an OBE asana.[28] Positions with the limbs straight may be better for blood circulation. Notice any physical tension you have and relax and release it. Mentally scan for tension and relax. One supplement is to tense the body as a whole to accentuate tension, and *then* relax. This tensing to start can result in a deeper relaxation faster, but don't overdo it.

Progressive Relaxation. Conversely you can progressively relax the body in sequence, for example in 12 parts: feet, calves, thighs, and hips; hands, forearms, biceps, and shoulders; abdomen, chest, neck, and head. Focus on the feet and relax them until they are completely relaxed. Then move onto the calves, etc. The tension supplement can be applied sequentially as well, for instance tensing the feet and then relaxing them, tensing the calves and then relaxing them, etcetera. Upon reaching the end of the sequence you can

---

[28] OBE asanas are covered in Chapter 9.

repeat the sequence, or attend to any parts that can still use some relaxation, as needed.

Triple Spheres Relaxation. Visualize a large sphere hovering over your body with the number 3 encased within it. Imagine the sphere composed of healing, relaxing, purging energy. Imagine the sphere floating down and entering and suffusing your body with healing and relaxation. Then imagine any heavy, tense, or negative energy sinking out of your body into the floor, through the structure of the building (away from any people, animals, or plants), and harmlessly into the ground. Imagine three number 3 spheres, two number 2 spheres, and one number 1 sphere.

MEDITATION

Meditation has many forms and types and definitions. For the purposes of the out-of-body experience basic I define meditation as the technical slowing down and calming of the body and the mind. This naturally induces an altered state. Without some basic ability to concentrate meditation devolves into daydreaming, reverie, or simply falling sleep. Without some ability to relax you may find yourself just sitting there. A conscious, relaxed, altered state (alpha, theta, or delta) can be called a meditative state or trance state. Alpha can be considered a *light trance*, theta a *full trance*, and delta a *deep trance*. I suggest practicing at least once or twice a day. A good meditation session is 10 or 15 minutes long.

4-2 Rhythmic Breathing Meditation. Sit comfortably and inhale to the mental count of 4, hold the lungs full to the mental count of 2, exhale to the mental count of 4, and then hold the lungs empty to the mental count of 2. Repeat this sequence of breathing, with a *steady rhythm* however fast or slow, relaxing as you do so but keeping good posture. As you continue and start entering altered states it will be harder to maintain the rhythm, at which point you can let the rhythm go and simply sit in the mental and physical stillness of the altered state.

Mantra Meditation. Pick a short phrase or a set of syllables to mentally repeat. A common one is the syllable "Om." Another mantra which I've used successfully is "La-Ra-SS." Usually the syllable or set of syllables are drawn out. So for "Om" it's mentally chanted as "Oooooohhhhhhhhhmmmmmmmmm." And for "La-Ra-Ss" it's "Laaaahhhhhh... Rrrrrrraaaaaaaahhhhh... SSsssssss." Simply sit and mentally repeat the word or phrase. It may help to start the mantra verbally, and when the pattern is established gradually switch to mental chanting. Just as with the rhythmic breathing meditation, when you start to enter altered states you can let go of the mantra and sit in stillness.

VISUALIZATION

Visualization is important to developing out-of-body experience capability because it helps develop the perceptual mechanism used while in the out-of-body experience. Visualizing is a good warm-up to OBE practice sessions. We've already covered the *Concentration-Visualization* exercise in the Concentration section. That exercise is sufficient to practice visualizing, but here is another. As you get more skilled at concentration and visualization, or as a close to your session, you can practice visualization exercises with eyes open.

Visualize a Shape. Set a 5-minute timer, close your eyes, and hold visualization of any geometric shape of your choosing. You may want to periodically spin and turn the shape as you visualize, to help keep your attention focused and to keep a single shape and single color. You may experience your attention wavering or the shape changing –

simply bring it back to your original shape and color and position of choice.

MENTAL PROJECTION

Mental projection or mind shifting is a form of out-of-body experiencing whereby you focus your intention on perceiving from a different point in time-space, resulting in experiencing yourself there like viewing a feed from a roaming camera. With practice, and with extended maintenance of the shift, more and more of oneself is shifted until ultimately it can become an out-of-body experience proper. Memory, imagination, and a sense of actually being at the new location may all play a part at first. Gradually the experience becomes more and more practical and objective. Simply imagine a place and focus on imagining it as if you are there, floating like an invisible eye. Start with a place you know well. You may find that you discover something new about the area, or find someone visiting that you can later confirm visited at that time. Mental projection has immediate use to help finding lost items. You can imagine the item, and then move your mind-shifted perspective back from the object and *see* where the item is located. What is it sitting next to? Pull perspective back further; where is it? When you succeed the effectiveness of this can be startling. Mental projection is also a good technique to add to any OBE practice session, and as a warm-up to any session.

ENERGY WORKING

Energy working is the practice of consciously stimulating or manipulating the energy body. Versions of energy working practices you may have heard of include chi gung/qi gong, shiatsu, acupuncture, reiki, and the like. It only takes 15 or 20 minutes for a good energy working session. It takes concentration to make it through a session. The practice can also lead to altered state markers such as vibrations and various energy sensations. In altered states energy flow is stronger, and conversely energy working, by increasing energy flow, can lead to altered states. And simply that it is an inwardly or nonphysically focused practice lends itself to altered states. Increasing energy flow regularly through energy work can assimilate the energy body to increased activity and decrease or eliminate uncomfortable energy sensations during trance work.

Energy working can be done utilizing any of the senses, while the primary three I use are tactile imagery (touch), visual imagery (sight), and auditory imagery (sound). Each I think has its uses and benefits, though I've focused mostly on tactile and visual methods. Be gentle and patient with your energy working, to not overload the energy circuits. I had an experience where I purposely tactilely overstimulated my crown and brow chakras as an experiment, and I experienced a burning sensation as if someone poured hot grease or hot oil onto my head that rolled down to my brow. For several days just to think of my scalp or brow brought a sensation of sizzling, so I spent the time avoiding thinking about these areas as they healed.

TACTILE IMAGING

A simple way to tactilely stimulate the energy body is to move your awareness through your body. The energy body is both a field of energy, as well as a conglomeration of energy conduits called *meridians* that are similar to the physical circulatory system. Moving your intention through the energy body both stimulates the substance of the energy body and increases and clears the flow of energy through the meridians. You can progressively stimulate the energy body along the same sequence as the progressive relaxation exercise shared in the Relaxation basic section. Start with one of your feet, and move your awareness through your foot, from your toes to your heel, back and forth, as if moving a sponge or a ball of energy back and forth through your foot. After some time of doing this you should feel tingling or other energetic sensations. Then move to the other foot and repeat, and then continue with the calves, thighs, etcetera, until you end up moving awareness through your head. After going through each body part in turn you can move energy back and forth through the body as a whole, from the feet through and to the head, back and forth. One or two repetitions of this entire sequence would be sufficient as an energy working session. As you get better you can try both feet simultaneously, etcetera, and increase to broader areas of stimulation at the start.

You can also refine the practice by directly stimulating specific energy centers, called *chakras*. Chakras are to the energy body as organs are to the physical body. Stimulating chakras heals and strengthens the energy body. You can stir your awareness through the area of a chakra, like drawing a swirl onto a piece of paper with your mind and intention. We can categorize the chakras as *primary*, *major*, and *minor*.

The *primary chakras* are located along the centerline of the body, and each of the primary chakras has front and rear counterparts, 14 primary chakras in total. These include the (14) crown chakra across the top of the head and (1) the root chakra, its counterpart, at the perineum between the anus and genitals; (2) the sex chakra above the genitals at the pubic bone and (3) its counterpart at the base of the spine; (4) the navel chakra a few inches below the navel and (5) its counterpart at the same height on the back; (6) the solar plexus chakra at the center of the solar plexus and (7) its counterpart at the same height on the back; (8) the heart chakra in the center of the chest and (9) its counterpart at its opposition position on the back; (10) the throat chakra in front of the throat and (11) its counterpart at the back of the neck; (12) the "third eye" in between the eyebrows and (13) its counterpart at the same height on the back of the head.

There is a *major chakra* in the center of the palm of each hand, and in the center of the sole of each foot. You can stir your awareness through these to stimulate them, just as you do with the primary chakras. There are also energy storage centers throughout the body, areas for the collection of energy. There is one in the direct center of the head, one in the direct center of the chest, with the primary energy storage center in the direct center of the body at a height of a few inches below the navel, encompassing the entire area of the physical intestines. This storage center is called the *dan tien* in Chinese energy arts. You can simply focus there and allow energy to collect, center, and build, and feel heat, coolness, tingling, or other sensation as the energy builds. You can also use your mind and intention like an energy sponge to repeatedly draw or scoop energy into this center; up your legs and/or arms, through your body, to this center. You can also go around or through the head as you bring the energy from the limbs, up your back, around your head, and down to the primary energy storage center. Another way to build and store energy is with deep breathing, breathing deeply and then emptying the lugs fully with continued intention into the dan tien region.

To combine the practices of energy body stimulation and increasing energy stores, you can draw or sponge energy up your legs through your feet, and into your root chakra. After drawing energy there several times you can stir the root chakra with your intention. Then you can draw energy through your feet up your legs *through* the root chakra and into the rear sex chakra. Repeat drawing energy into the rear sex chakra several times, and then stir the rear sex chakra. Then repeat the energy draw and stirring through to the next primary chakra, and the next, up the rear chakra line and then down the front chakra line. After finishing all primary chakras you can just repeatedly draw energy up the legs into the root chakra, up the spine, down the front centerline back to the root chakra, and then up into the lower storage center.

There are *minor chakras* at the tips of each finger and at the tips of each toe. Ten of the major meridians of the energy body begin and end at these minor chakras. One way to utilize the major chakras of the hands and feet and the minor chakras of the fingers and toes to draw and build energy is to simply focus on the tips of the fingers and the palms of the hand to stimulate those chakras. Do the same with the tips of the toes and the soles of the feet. Then breathe deeply, with full inhales and exhales, with the intention that energy is automatically drawn into your hands and feet. In this practice it isn't necessary to move your intention like scooping energy. Simply focus on the chakras of the hands and feet, breathe, and allow energy to build. This is a great practice to do outdoors in natural settings.

The most widely known feature of the energy body is likely the aura, the energy egg that accompanies everything. Stimulation and strengthening of the aura can be done by simply feeling an oval egg of energy surrounding the body, and feeling it to be strong, energetic, vibrant, and robust. Within the aura are what have been called "health lines," a multitude of energy spikes that extend from the body outwards in all directions, like spokes stretching out from the center of a wheel. You can imagine the sensation of tactilely *combing* these lines outward with your intention, as if combing your fingers through hair, so that they stand straight and tall outwards from the body.

VISUAL IMAGING

Visualization to stimulate the energy body is as simple as visualizing the energy centers and structures of the body, as well as visualizing the drawing, building, or movement of energy. Different colors are associated with the different primary energy centers. Generally speaking: deep red for the root chakra, red for the sex chakras, orange for the navel chakras, yellow for the solar plexus chakras, green for the heart chakras, blue for the throat chakras, indigo or dark blue for the brow or "third eye" chakras, and violet or purple for the crown chakra. You can simply visualize the chakra glowing the appropriate color, progressively visualizing all of the primary chakras in succession. You can also visualize the flows of energy up the limbs and into the primary chakras, or into the storage center.

AUDITORY IMAGING

Using sound to stimulate the energy body is something I don't have as much experience with, but have experimented with. Apparently vowel sounds correspond to different chakras – "O" with the heart chakra, "I" with the brow or third eye chakra, and "E" with the throat chakra. The heart chakra has been linked with greater compassion and openness, so intoning O is to help stimulate this. The third eye has been linked with psychic functioning and clairvoyance, so intoning "I" is to stimulate this. The throat chakra is associated with telepathy and mental transmissions, and intoning "E" is to stimulate this. Practice of verbally intoning these sounds has a definite and immediate stimulation of the associated chakra for me, but how much actually focusing on the chakra while intoning has an effect versus the intoning itself is unknown to me.

ENERGY EXCHANGE

We routinely exchange energy with the environment, including the natural environment and other people. Just like how we live in a sea of air, and constantly inhale and exhale air, exchanging it amongst each other, animals, plants, and other life – including nowadays our machinery, we exchange energy as well. Whereas some people impart neutral interactions, and others impart a mutual sense of uplifting, there are also those who have negative impacts upon our energy, drawing and stealing energy with no return of energy. We've experienced interactions with people who leave us feeling depleted. Perhaps they unload sad stories of their trials and tribulations, and after departing we feel low and drained – and sometimes we can see that person looking visibly energized as they depart. Some people are actually energy vampires, who either consciously or unconsciously steal energy from others.

I remember running into an energy vampire at work one day, a lady who was jealous of my plans to write books and do various things in the world. She sat next to me at work, and at the end of her shift I suddenly started to feel very heavy and sleepy; so much so that I ended up sitting back in my chair in the middle of my work day and closing my eyes, feeling like if I just shut down a bit I might feel better. After seemingly dozing off a bit, I was alerted by her getting up and walking towards the exit. But she was walking as if she was overflowing with energy to the point being unable to control her gait. I reviewed the situation and saw the telltale signs of a vampire attack. I felt sleepy and listless, while afterwards she was perceivably energized. The way she arranged her hair was even reminiscent of an energy vampire. It was wild and arranged as if a conglomeration of tentacles, quite similar in appearance to the documented shape of the auras of energy vampires by Joe Slate in his book *Psychic Vampires*. An energy vampire's aura develops dark pointy tentacles, which are used to actually pierce the energy auras of their victims.

The next day this lady came into work talking about all the ideas she had for writing and creative endeavors, and how it was going to be "big," and she told me that she "got it off you." And that afternoon she tried to energy attack me again. Being aware of the situation and using my learning from *Psychic Vampires* to shield myself I was prepared. I felt the telltale sensations of an attack – I felt a gentle prick in the vicinity of the upper left area of my aura (she was sitting to my left), and I felt the draw or drain of energy, and the sensation of getting sleepy and lightheaded. I closed my eyes, interlocked my fingers, and imagined and intended my aura to be vibrant, strong, and shielded, with a bright impenetrable field of light protecting it. The hand position taught by Slate, which I'll call the *Interlocking Ring Mudra*, is done by first making a ring with the fingers by touching the tips of the thumb and middle finger together – one ring with the thumb and middle finger of your right hand, and another ring with the thumb and middle finger of the left hand. And then *interlock the two finger rings*. Open one of the rings and reclose it *within* the other ring loop. Maintain the fingers interlocked in this way as you visualize your aura being strong, vibrant, and shielding.

I felt the attack halt immediately, and the lady stood up abruptly and looked over the cubicle wall at me with a surprised look on her face, carrying her prickly looking, full and wild head of hair up with her. Hearing her move I looked up and over to the left, and caught her quizzically staring directly at me. She sat back down and I turned straight to continue my defense. Sure enough she tried again to energy drain me. Again, after some time, she popped up and looked at me quizzically over the cubicle wall, with me again looking up and over to catch her as she did. She got up and left work, and I avoided sitting close to her after that day. The next day when she came into work I very visibly avoided sitting next to her, looking at her as I found a seat far away from her. She was watching me, and we passed a knowing look between each other.

Energy vampirism also occurs through use of the out-of-body experience state. One time I researched an organization engaged in energy vampirism. I was always intrigued with the vampire mythos in movies and cinema, and according to this group the movie version of the blood sucking vampire is actually an amalgamation of the "true" vampire that sucks energy instead of physical blood. After hearing one of their officials conduct an interview on a popular radio show I bought their official book, and soon learned that their representative lied on the show about their practices. He said they just take ambient energy from people, but their book clearly directs their adherents in the taking of energy until full, regardless of the effect upon the victim, who they deem to be less evolved than and a lower species than "vampires." I decided to not take up this practice, but in buying the book I must have come to their attention. Their book describes not only sucking energy from people in physical proximity, like with my work experience of an energy vampire, but also at higher skill levels sucking energy from people by traveling to them via the out-of-body state. This, they claimed, accounted for the accounts of vampires not being visible in mirrors, being able to fly, and being able to disappear. According to them the vampire was in the out-of-body state.

One day sitting in my apartment I became acutely aware that a nonphysical being had entered the room. I looked in its direction, and then felt the signature sensation of my energy being tapped by an outside source; that subtle pinch, with a corresponding loss of energy. I applied the same shielding tactic, which halted the attack immediately, and soon the being left never to be heard from again.

That organization of people erroneously believes it makes them better and stronger than other people to steal their energy, when in fact as Joe Slate found out through rigorous empirical investigation, the practice of energy vampirism only weakens the energy system, resulting in greater need to steal energy, perpetuating more weakening, and on and on, in a debilitating downward spiral.

Some energy interactions are even more subtle. I remember standing on a public bus one day, and feeling an energy tentacle moving towards me and connecting with my root chakra. I looking around searching, sensing for the source, and as I looked at a male sitting to my left I felt the energy tubule withdraw abruptly as he suddenly looked visibly discomforted or embarrassed and looked away from me. I had the distinct impression that he was a young gay man who was attracted to me and had been thinking intently on me before I looked his way.

There are other energy exchanges that are extremely beneficial and healing in nature. Two great examples are Barbara Brennan, author of *Hands of Light*, and Choa Kok Sui, author of *Pranic Healing*. They both teach and practice using energy and the energy body to heal oneself and others of all kinds of illness and ailments. Barbara Brennan also offers a very detailed and multidimensionally intricate analysis of the energy body.

AWARENESS

Awareness is a form of concentration, where rather than focusing on a single object, you remain generally focused on the activity or environment of the moment, ignoring distracting imagination and reverie. This practice is *not* meant to be absolute – the occasional extraneous thought is welcome, and can be a form of guidance from a higher source, or recall of a needed piece of information, or something to be addressed in whatever way. It's not a practice of denial or repression. Awareness is about eliminating unproductive and unconstructive lapses of attention – *extraneous and purposeless wandering of mind is what this practice curtails.*

Awareness Walks / Drives / Etc. A good way to fit this practice in is to practice during travels. You can go on a walk, or if you drive regularly carve out a portion of your drive – 15 minutes is a good start, and for this duration remain acutely aware of the sights, sounds, smells, etc., that are there for you to experience as you walk/drive. Let the full experience of the walk/drive engulf your entire awareness. If you start to daydream come back to the here and now. Be aware of your environment, your body, and the clear conscious awareness of a silent and present mind. This practice will help with general clarity and awareness during the OBE – as well as during life. You may find during these times you drive better, or are less likely to trip when walking!

Awareness Tasks. Another way to practice awareness is to spend time on one task. Start small. If you have a certain task to complete, for instance to wash the dishes, try focusing on washing the dishes, bringing your mind back from daydreams, reveries, dwelling on the past, anticipating the future, etcetera. Focus your full attention on washing the dishes until the dishes are complete. And if you must address something mentally, rather than addressing it *while* washing instead consciously take a moment and address it. Then you're practicing awareness on what you're addressing. It's about developing the ability to consciously dictate where your attention flows.

PSYCHIC DEVELOPMENT

A result of state acquisition progress is development of psychic abilities. And conversely, practicing psychic development helps develop state acquisition ability. As discussed, the altered states of alpha, theta, and delta are the states in which psychic perceptions are experienced. With the out-of-body experience altered state perceptions are usually had *to the exclusion of* physical world beta perceptions. Okanos called this *shifting*. With psychic functioning, altered state perceptions are had *in conjunction with* physical world beta perceptions. Okanos called this *expansion* or *expanding*. Whether it is clairvoyance, telepathy, psycho-metry, energy sensing, aura vision, telekinesis, channeling, or other life recall, these are abilities that can be explained as consciously entering hybrid altered states where one is conscious in the beta world *and* conscious in or consciously aware of higher dimensional worlds simultaneously. Consciously practicing psychic abilities as standalone practices will help develop your ability to enter altered states and to bring altered state perceptions and information back to conscious physical beta awareness.

CLAIRVOYANCE

Clairvoyance is the ability to perceive beyond the limits of physical eye perspective perception. This can include glimpses into other lifetimes, being aware of a happening far removed from your physical location, or awareness of a future event. You can help develop this ability by efforts to perceive beyond the physical range. The early stages of Mental Projection is a basic example of this – especially the exercise to find lost objects. *Remote viewing* is another example of clairvoyance – except with remote viewing various protocols are used to help screen extraneous perceptions and judgments that may cloud or taint clairvoyant perception. You can also try simple things like closing your eyes and imagining who is calling when the phone rings, or what color car is passing next while waiting at a red light on a highway.

TELEPATHY

Telepathy is the ability to perceive others' thoughts and make others aware of your thoughts. Telepathy is actually a very common ability and is instrumental to our everyday interactions, though largely on an unconscious level. When talking with someone you can relax and open your awareness, and be aware of information the person is sending on a nonphysical level. You may become aware of a subtle telepathic communication with aspects of the person's psyche he or she may not even be consciously aware of; and that you were heretofore unaware of in yourself! And if you have someone you can practice with you can try to send and receive colors, numbers, etc. If you find someone "on your mind" they could be thinking of you. You can relax and open to see what they are sending. You may learn of the topic of discussion before they call to tell you about it. Or if you'd rather not be bothered you can send the person love and then focus back on what you were doing, to shield yourself from unwanted telepathic messages and attentions. [29]

PSYCHOMETRY

Psychometry is the ability to sense the vibrations imprinted upon objects by events and by the beings handling or near the object. For instance, practice holding a used book and relaxing and opening yourself to perceive what vibrations may be stored therein. This may allow you to perceive the

---

[29] These are tips on telepathy from the Orin book *Personal Power through Awareness*.

emotions a previous reader experienced while reading the book, or to become aware of where the book has been.

ENERGY SENSING

Energy sensing is simply being aware of the vibrations of an area. We have all experienced entering a room and being aware of the excited energy in the room or the depressing energy of the room. The ability can be developed to sense even subtle changes in the energetic environment. Open yourself to sense the nature of the energy as you enter a room, or stand near a person, to practice this ability.

AURA VISION

Aura vision is the ability to perceive the auric field in and around beings and objects. Simply with a relaxed and diffused focus look around the edges of a living entity such as a human, animal, or plant, or even your own hand. Holding a relaxed, steady, and patient peripheral gaze you practice and develop this ability. You can also stimulate and focus on the brow chakra as a warm-up and during aura vision practice.

TELEKINESIS

Telekinesis is the ability to move objects by nonphysical means. A simple exercise to demonstrate this ability is to take a sewing needle and place it gently on the water in a glass full of water. The surface tension of the water will keep the needle afloat. Place your hands on the table or counter on either side of the glass and stare at the needle, and use your intent to make the needle spin. Another exercise is to take a square piece of paper or foil and make two diagonal creases through its center so that it's pointed in the center like the roof of a house. Then place it on a pointed object such as a pencil held upright between two books, and focus on making the "wheel" spin. Telekinesis practices can also be used as concentration exercises.

CHANNELING

Channeling is the practice of using altered states to access information from nonphysical sources, or through nonphysical means from a physical source, which can be your own higher self or intuition, extraterrestrials, spirit guides, or even our own past or future selves. A simply practice is to sit with pen and paper, or a word processing file, enter an altered state, and open to what information you can receive. If you would like a specific source, an extraterrestrial, a spirit guide, you can state this intention. If you will remember, this is how I met Okanos. You may start to get impressions, hear words, or see images, and your hands may start to spontaneously write or type – called automatic writing. Highly skilled channels whose work I admire include Helen Schucman, Lyssa Royal, Darryl Anka, and Adrian Dvir.

OTHER LIFE RECALL

Other life recall is the experience of becoming aware of details of other lifetimes one has. One exercise I devised that can help bring other lifetimes into awareness I'll call the **Trans-Incarnational Mirror Exercise**. Use the 4-2 Rhythmic Breathing Meditation to reach an alpha- to theta-level altered state. Imagine yourself in a vacant dimensional space standing before a large mirror. Look into the mirror and see yourself as you are now. Then imagine that as you look into the mirror, in the mirror's reflection standing behind you, you see a large grouping of people representing your other lives. Turn around and look at and interact with the personages of your other lifetimes.

9 – PRACTICAL CONSIDERATIONS

TIMINGS OF PRACTICE

Timings of practice can be very important. Any *time* of day or night is fine. This timing has to do with the state of your physiology and psychology. It's good to practice when drowsy; drowsiness helps you to go into sleep and thus enter altered states. If you apply techniques for a while and don't experience progress through the states try taking a break and practicing again when you feel drowsier. If you're too wide awake it may be harder to get into altered states. If you're too sleepy you may just fall asleep. If you regularly feel too sleepy when you practice try practicing earlier or getting more sleep overall. Remember the idea of *balance*. Ideally, riding the wave of our natural physiological calls to sleep and to awaken is good for state acquisition and metaphysical pursuits in general. We can use our wakefulness for physical pursuits and use our sleepiness for nonphysical pursuits.

Breaking wakefulness and sleep so that practice is dispersed throughout the day/night yields a fertile ground for state acquisition. This can be accomplished by practicing meditation, OBE, and altered state exercises throughout the day, and by waking to practice once or twice during the night. The practice of breaking the sleep period into two or more blocks has been called the *interrupted sleep technique*. One example is to set an alarm to wake you after 6 hours of sleep. And then, after staying up for 30 minutes to an hour, to practice OBE. The intervening time between sleep and practice is a good time to journal experiences, including dreams.

Another good time is to practice *as you awaken* for the day; especially if you awaken naturally. If you awake naturally endeavor to not arouse yourself but to go straight into an OBE technique. If you awaken by alarm hit the snooze button or reset the alarm if you must get up at a certain time, and then go into practice.

PRACTICE ENVIRONMENT

You can practice in any environment. The only limits will be determined by how well you can stay calm and focused in the environment. It's a good idea to change your location from your normal sleep location – if you normally sleep in bed practice OBE on a sofa, or on the living room floor on a blanket, for example. This will also help you to not just fall asleep. You can wake for interrupted sleep practice and then move to the sofa to practice OBE. Even simply changing orientation in bed – switching which side your head is on – can help.

Generally you want to be warm, as your body will cool as you relax and as your heartbeat and respiration slows. You may want to start practice slightly warmer than comfortable. You may find a layer or two of clothing and a light sheet more comfortable than a heavy blanket. Another variable is tolerable noise level. The environment can be as noisy as you can handle, but of course a quiet environment may be good to start with. Tolerance for uncomfortable variables increases as your skill increases.

OBE ASANAS

Asana is a word for the body positions of various yoga practices. Definite body positioning during OBE practice can be very supportive. While *it is not necessary to be in any specific position to practice OBE or altered states*, practice-specific positioning can help prep the mind for practice versus normal unconscious sleep. If you use practice positions that are sufficiently different from your normal sleep positioning, you can catch yourself during spontaneous OBEs by noticing you're suddenly out of that unusual position. I've for instance practiced with legs folded and suddenly realized my legs were straight. I had disconnected from the physical body and my nonphysical legs were straight.

It's *not* necessary to remain perfectly still during OBE or altered state practice. This is a common fallacy. You can move to scratch your nose, to get more comfortable, to shake off an uncomfortable altered state phenomenon, etc. After you do so simply go back to the practice. And of course you can also just remain still through any discomfort if you like. Ironically my moving to alleviate discomfort eventually evolved into *purposely* moving as an OBE technique, my trademark *relax-move technique,* which I'll describe in detail next chapter.

Another fallacy is that you can't cross your arms or legs during OBE practice. Doing so is *not* metaphysically dangerous in any way, as I've had experiences with arms crossed several times. Also you *can* wear jewelry and any type of clothing, but you may be *more comfortable* without jewelry and with loose fitting clothing, or without any clothing at all.

The general rule with positioning is a basic degree of warmth and comfort; or controlled discomfort. Sometimes an unusual position can help you remain aware. If you utilize any of these poses you may find variations of them that work better for you. First are the images of the asana, and then the description.

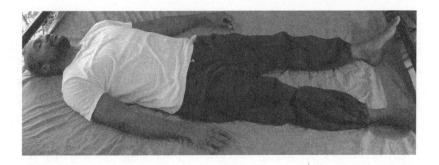

Plank Pose. Flat on the back, legs and arms outstretched. Arms and hands can also lay folded across the abdomen or chest. Legs can instead be folded at 90 degree angles so that the feet are flat, with the knees in the air, the legs two upward pointing triangles. Or the feet can be placed soles together, making a diamond shape of the legs.

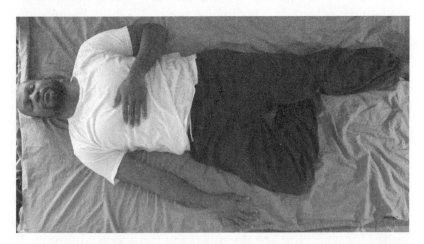

Z-Pose. For the right side: Start in basic Plank Pose, and then the right leg is folded underneath the left knee, with the right calf or right ankle under the left knee. Also the right sole can be placed against the inner side of the left knee. Place the left arm folded across the chest.

Sleep-Comfortable Pose. Get into any position that you use to go to sleep, as if you're really only going to sleep. This position (if used at all) is best utilized midway or later in the practice session, to help finish the shift into the OBE. When you're just starting this pose may have you just fall asleep!! Wait until you can maintain a reasonable trance for a duration of time before trying this one!

Egyptian Pose. Sitting on a chair or structure, feet flat on the floor, palms on the knees or thighs, or hands in a mudra.

Dorsal Pose. Just like Plank Pose but faced downward, stomach towards the floor, arms at the sides, and face to the side. Variations include the arms above the head as if making a "U," with arms outstretched to the sides making a "T," or one arm up and one arm down.

Folded Pose. Fold your arms across your chest, and also fold your legs at the ankles or calves. I've found this position best when on my side. This pose can arouse lucidity in dreams by the experience of restriction of movement in your dream limbs.

Indian Pose. This is the classic folded-leg pose. Sitting cross-legged, palms on the knees, or hands in a mudra resting on the knees or thighs.

OBE Mudras

Mudras are asanas for the hands. Certain hand positions are more amenable to certain flows of energy. And certain types of intent, or certain types of focus, consistently correlate with different hand and finger configurations. This is empirically discernable. The idea is that there are 12 major *meridians* or energy lines of the nonphysical body, and 10 of them start/end in the minor chakras at the tips of fingers and toes.[30] When the hands and fingers are interlocked in certain ways, certain energy lines are directly connected; while other lines are not directly connected. And certain connections of the energy body coincide with certain energy states, physical states, and psychological states. Here are some hand positions I've discovered, developed, or researched, that can help you in your practices. First are the images of the mudra, and then the description.

---

[30] 11 and 12 are at the centerline of the body going through the front primary chakras and the rear primary chakras. Together they are the main channel or main circuit in Chinese energy systems, with energy usually going up the spine, around the head, down the front center line, around the perineum, and back up the spine in a continuous circuit. Touch the tongue to the roof of the mouth to complete this circuit. You can practice running energy through this circuit to experience Kundalini energy, a spurt or geyser of energy up the spine. Periodically run the energy in reverse to balance the flow. There are also belt meridians or belt channels going horizontally through the primary chakras, for instance horizontally around the head going through the front and rear brow chakras, horizontally around the neck going through the front and real throat chakras, etc.

DEBJ Mudra. Notice that the tips of the thumbs are resting in the first or tip joint crease of the pointer finger. The other fingers have a wide 130 degree curve. The hands can be rested in whatever way they comfortably fall on the legs or knees for sitting positions, or on the resting surface if lying down. This mudra is great for deep altered states and general meditation.

Fire Mudra. Start with the Finger-Clasp Mudra, and then point the pointer fingers, placing them against each other. My experience is that this mudra is good for concentration practice and attentive or active mental states.

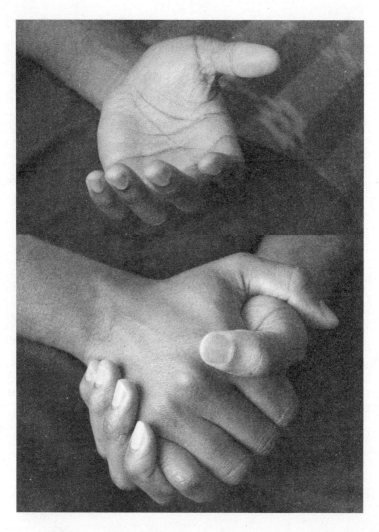

Angle Clasp Mudra. The hands are clasped perpendicular to each other, with either hand on top as is comfortable. I suggest starting with your dominant hand on top. This is a great mudra for rest and relaxation.

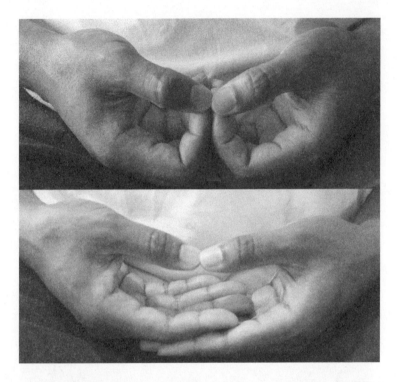

Buddha's Mudra. These are hand positions similar to those I've seen in many Buddha statues. The thumbs touch, and the fingers are either curved with backs touching or laying on top of each other. This mudra is great for sitting positions and energy working sessions.

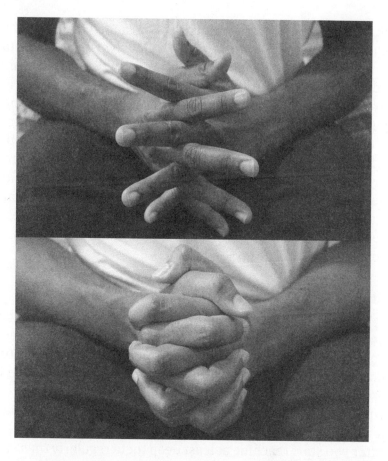

Finger-Clasp Mudra. This is a great general mudra. The hands are placed palm together with fingers interlocked, and then the hands simply clasp together. A very restful hand position.

JOURNALING

Keep track of what occurs as you practice. Journaling is important early on. With practice you'll be able to anticipate your commonly experienced state acquisition phenomenon, or your *signature phenomena*. In time you'll see what state markers occur for you regularly. Journaling will also help cultivate a mental environment conducive to altered state practice, as well as helping recall of occurrences. Journaling your practice sessions can be a fun, motivational, focusing, and extremely rewarding practice. Even just a two liner about what happened is a good start. The more detailed the better.

General components include date and time of practice, what technique(s) you used – or will use if starting the entry prior to practice, the start and end time of practice, and a detailed account of what occurred during the session. You may also add afterthoughts, which may include any hypotheses or conclusions about your experiences, and any ideas or correlations you make.

GOALS AND MOTIVATIONS

Having a goal in mind for your OBE can mobilize your energy, motivation, and focus. Before practice you can recall and affirm the goal, and practice with intent to achieve it. Goals don't have to be very tight and focused. It could be just to fly around and then reenter the physical state. I suggest starting with reaching certain altered state plateaus. Reach alpha daily for a week or two, and then theta the next week or two, etc. After you start reaching at least deep theta regularly *then* start attempting to cause OBEs. This idea is very practical, and can eliminate much frustration at perceived failure by giving you time to develop enough flexibility of consciousness to be able to achieve a consciously initiated OBE. After you start achieving OBEs a simple goal could be increased OBE count. Intend to get at least one more OBE than you did the month before. Don't be upset or beat yourself up if you fail to reach whatever goal you set. But congratulate yourself for the effort and drive. With continued practice you will succeed.

CHECKLISTS, GRAPHS, AND CHARTS

Checklists, graphs, and charts can help with goals and motivation. You can make a checklist for the basic practice techniques as well as to check off how many OBE practices you do, OBE successes, deepest state reached for the day, etcetera. This can be very motivational – see if you can get in more practices this week than you did the previous, or this *day* than you did the previous. You can look and see the foundation of effort you're building as you move forward and see a sheet filled more and more with tick marks. And with each practice, each check, you get better and closer to OBE success and/or greater OBE proficiency. Just be sure not to be down on yourself if you *don't* fill every box with a tick mark. If a checklist proves too hard to complete perhaps you can discontinue trying to use one, or make a checklist with fewer items.

Here's a sample checklist listing the month and year and day, several basics practices, number of OBE practices, deepest altered state reached, and number of OBE successes. The data from such a sheet can be turned into a chart or graph for visual representation:

Month/Year	Med	Relax	Conc	E-Work	OBE Pract	Deepest State Reached	# of OBEs
1							
2							
3							
4..5.. Etc.							

PSYCHOLOGICAL PREP FOR OBE

It's so easy to get so caught up in the happenings of the beta physical dimension that the leftover time, energy, thought, and effort we put into OBE practices are insufficient to generate success. My many periods of downtime from OBE practice usually involved hyper involvement in physical world life. When engrossed in physical world life even a minute of concentration practice can seem like too great a loss; like too much time to detract from our physical world 'hustle and bustle.' OBE progress may involve *slowing down* mentally, and withdrawing psychologically from the fast paced, mind-numbing magnetism of the daily grind. It may require eliminating unnecessary, stressful, or time consuming preoccupations.

Committing to a gradually more robust checklist can have sufficient attention freed from fourth dimensional addiction. Perhaps commit to at least one basics practice a day, and one OBE practice day, the same day of the week. It's common to start practice with a flurry of activity, only for activity to taper off drastically after a few weeks. Try a gradually building mental space for it instead. Ride the wave of wakefulness and sleepiness to help maintain a natural balance between waking and altered states practice. Both your physical life and your nonphysical life will be the better for it! Being rested physically we operate better in the physical world. And having attended to our physical concerns effectively we're less mentally preoccupied when practice time comes. Also remember the preparatory breathing exercise offered in the Basics Prep section (Chapter 8).

PHYSIOLOGICAL PREP FOR OBE

Being either half full to on an empty stomach I find is best. You can get into different positions more easily, and it just feels more comfortable to be lighter. Stretching helps as well, especially a nice and slow stretching routine like Yoga. It can be a good warm-up before practice. A warm bath or shower helps as well. It cleanses the body and the pores, and warms up the muscles and helps with blood flow. The better your blood flow the less discomfort you'll feel as your heartbeat and respiration slows down during trance. Thus regular stretching and exercise while not mandatory to success are definitely a plus. Some instances of discomfort during altered state practice are rather than altered state phenomenon just signs of neglect of physical maintenance.

It's also beneficial to place your limbs in a stretched position if the limb is straight. For instance if in Plank Pose with arms at the side, lift and stretch your arms and legs towards the foot of the bed (or whatever surface you're practicing on), and then set them down so they are slightly held stretched by the friction of the bed. Don't overdo it, but a slight stretch may help ease blood flow and decrease any sense of constriction.

PATIENT PERSISTENCE

Chances are you won't succeed the first time you attempt to OBE – you may not even experience any substantial alpha state phenomenon the first time you practice state acquisition. Keep going and don't get discouraged. As you practice and start to experience altered state phenomenon, intend to get at least to where you have gotten in your previous practice. I suggest the measured approach of reaching alpha each day for a week, and then theta each day for a week, etcetera. Only progress to the next state after 7 days of consistent success.

A month of patient, consistent, progressive practice one hour per day will trump a 24 hour day of practice once per month. And of course, if *in addition to* consistent practice you periodically spend an entire day or night practicing it can only help. Some of my greatest successes and most fun have been in binge nights of practicing OBE. But *consistent practice is key and the foundation of success.*

Patience helps even during each individual practice session. If you simply go along patiently, not trying to achieve the end result of an OBE immediately, you can remain more relaxed. And you may find much to your surprise that before you even realize it you have undocked from physical awareness and are in an OBE! By being patient and consistent states it may have taken an hour to reach initially start to take minutes to achieve.

10 – PRACTICING OBE

Now you have the basics, and practical considerations to support your practice. Here we get into actually initiating an out-of-body experience. This methodology has been tried and proven, and all you have to do is apply it as outlined and you will succeed at achieving out-of-body success.

CENTERING PREPARATION

Especially if you have a busy waking life, it may be very necessary to spend some time preparing to practice OBE. It can be likened to the time spent by a deep sea diver in a decompression chamber, preparing to reenter a different pressure environment. In this case it's not that any harm will come to you if you *don't* spend some time preparing. It's simply that if your attention and energies are still focused on and diffused into physical world concerns you may find that you have little or slow success at your OBE progress.

I suggest always starting any practice with the preparation of a few deep breaths – two or three full inhales with emptying and relaxing exhales. This will gradually become a sort of mental marker that you are beginning to engage different regions of yourself and the universe, and will prep your mind for the task. Lean your head backwards in the inhale, and tip your head forward on the exhale. Then spend a few minutes centering into the current moment, and the current place. Withdraw and center all of your energy and attention behind your current effort.

To help with this centering you can resolve any matters that can easily be resolved. Make sure all the doors and windows are secure – which is important so you don't mistake a nonphysical being to be a physical intruder! Make sure the stove is off. Be sure your work alarm is set – double check it! Make sure the kids are to bed. Make sure your homework is done. Make sure you've used the restroom. Anything that may take your attention away from the present place and time, if it can easily be resolved, resolve it. Things that can't immediately be resolved be sure to mentally delegate to another time. This can help with interrupted sleep practice, as you can delegate some things to do during the time between practices, to help you to get up.

OBE TECHNIQUES AND ROUTINES

I have found much success in using a barrage of techniques in succession, making a practice routine or *projection sequence*. I'll list techniques and then list various ways you can link them in your OBE practice sessions. I have also found great success in breaking practice sessions into two parts: sitting phase and lying phase. Start with a sitting phase using one of the sitting OBE Asanas and hit at least the alpha state while you are upright, so that you have made some progress into altered states before you lie down. This can help lessen the amount of times you fall asleep during practice. And then lie down and continue your practice session.

I have found it a great help to have an alarm or timer set marking the duration of each technique. 10 minutes per technique is a good interval, but be sure to vary it to what suits you. I would suggest no less than 10 minutes on each technique to not experience being too scattered among techniques. Two to four techniques is good to start with – for instance one until you hit alpha, and then another until you hit theta, and then one or two in combination until you hit delta and the OBE. 10 to 30 minutes total should be sufficient for the sitting phase, with 10 or 15 minutes allotted to each technique. *Recheck to make sure you set the alarm property before you start.* Then after sitting practice lie down, and continue or repeat the technique sequence.

As a general rule of thumb, if you seem relatively aware or awake, have a relaxed focus in your practice to allow yourself to descend into the altered states, and if you're relatively drowsy or sleepy, focus more strongly, to remain consciously aware as you descend into altered states. Focus as strongly as necessary to remain consciously aware, yet practice being physically and psychologically relaxed enough to go into sleep. If you pop alert and realize you had lost awareness or fell into unconscious reverie focus more strongly on the technique.

One powerful thing you can do as you practice is to *periodically check the depth of your state.* Take a moment to observe how relaxed the physical body is, and how deep you are into altered states. Observe what altered state markers are going on. Make a mental account of how much progress you are making during the session. This can go a long way towards keeping you consciously aware, as well as help motivate your progress during that session and future sessions. Sometimes it may not be readily apparent how deeply we enter into altered states until we really pay attention to what is going on and acknowledge each little progress and success.

MEDITATION TECHNIQUES

4-2 Rhythmic Breathing, Sitting in Stillness

You'll remember this from the Meditation basic. Inhale to the count of 4, hold the lungs full to the count of 2, exhale to the count of 4, and hold the lungs empty to the count of 2, repeat. This is usually the "bread and butter" of my practice session. I suggest always sitting and starting with this one to open the practice session. After you enter at least alpha let go of the rhythm and sit in stillness. You can easily hit theta with just this technique.

50-1 Countdown

Mentally count down repeatedly from 50-1. You can also visualize the number as you mentally say them. Relax as you do so. This is my friend Louis' "bread and butter" technique.

Awareness/Mindfulness

Just remain aware – remain aware of the sounds, temperatures, smells, etc., aware of your body, your breathing, your heartbeat, aware of your perceptions and experiences as you go through the altered states, aware of awareness itself. Simply remain psychologically aware as best you can. Let your mind be an open space, simply noticing each and every perception as it arises.

Belly Breathing

Relax and consciously breathe deeply with the belly/abdomen, with slow, full inhales and exhales. It can help to rest one hand on the chest and the other on the abdomen, and confirm that the abdomen is starting the inhales and ending the exhales.

Century Breath Count

You'll remember this from the Concentration basic. Simply count your breaths from 1 to 100. If you lose awareness or count, restart from 1 and focus more on the breath and the numbers. Remain as relaxed as possible. You can place a hand on the chest and the other on the abdomen to help you breathe and focus.

Energy Awareness/Sensing

Feel the energy in your body, and simply be aware of the energy. Feel the energy move and build as you allow yourself to go deeper into altered states. This is a great technique to switch to if you experience any kind of energetic sensation altered state phenomenon.

Mind Blank / Movie Screen

Simply blank the mind like an empty slate, or as if waiting for thunder after a lightning strike, or waiting for a movie to start on a blank cinema screen. Note – the experience of projection can be sudden with this technique.

Relax-Move Technique

This is a signature technique of mine. It can produce a very direct and powerful out-of-body experience. Every minute or two (the time can be adjusted to preference) move into a different physical position or OBE asana. This technique helps keep awareness intact, as well as provides an in-built movement protocol to initiate the out-of-body experience when your state is deep enough. You may go to move one time and realize that you're paralyzed. Then you can relax and roll out into an OBE. Deeply relax in-between each movement, or apply any other technique in-between movement. You can sit up or look over to check the time. You can make a brief journal entry. You can get more comfortable. Any type of physical movement will do.

Sleep Signal Focus

The sensation of sleepiness can be a fixative to concentrate upon. Become aware of or imagine the sensation of sleepiness and dive into it. This is a great technique to use if you start feeling extremely sleepy during practice. You can attempt to 'stay ahead' of sleepiness, diving into and keeping awareness ahead of it before it drowns you in unawareness. This is a signature technique of my friend Louis.

Slow Down

Relax and focus on slowing the heartbeat and/or respiration. Consciously intend and will and relax into the body slowing down.

State Marker Focus

Whatever state marker phenomenon you experience, you can simply focus on that to deepen and/or maintain your state. If you experience more than one state marker at a time you may want to focus on one. So for instance with visual imagery and energy sensations at the same time, it may be easier to focus on one or the other.

X-Ray Vision

Attempt to see *through* your eyelids, either into the immediate environment, or to a more distant time or place.

ENERGY WORKING TECHNIQUES

Chakra Focus

Focus on one of the chakra centers. You can simply focus intention on it, visualize it, or stir or spin your awareness through it. Be gentle so as not to overstimulate.

Energy Working

Practice energy working exercises, any or all of them. See Chapter 8.

Vibration Strobe

If you experience strong vibrations you can focus on them, relaxing into them, and then move them up and down your body. Intend them into the shape of a ring, like a thick hoop around your body, and move this hoop up and down from head level to feet level, back and forth. Energetic sensations often turn into vibrations, so you may find success switching to this technique after Energy Working or Energy Awareness/Sensing technique application. Vibration strobe can cause a spontaneous experience of floating up out of the body.

PHYSICAL DETACHMENT TECHNIQUES

Arm-Up

Lay on your back and place a forearm in the air at the elbow, so that the forearm is balanced in the air. When you reach a deep enough state your physical forearm may fall while you remain consciously aware and nonphysical. If you just lose awareness your falling arm can alert you back to practice. You can practice any other techniques or technique sequence while applying this. It may help you to remain aware far past your threshold so you can experience *extreme* sleepiness practicing this technique.

Dispersal

Image your physical body and/or psychological being dispersing. You can imagine for instance your body dispersing into a cloud of tiny spheres, which then floats into the air, or condenses and rolls down the bed and out along the floor like spilled water.

Displacement

Imagine yourself to be in a position, or facing a direction, other than the one you are physically in. In addition *from this imagined position* you can apply other OBE techniques. Imagine that your displaced position is actually your physical position.

Ident Method

This is a way to experience going directly to a destination or target (person, event, place, etc.). Take into your mind all you know of or feel for the destination or target – look, smell, sound, emotion, and etcetera – and hold it all in your mind as fully as you can with intent to go there. If you don't have personal knowledge of the target simply will to go to your intended destination.

Imagined Movement

Imagine movement, recreating the sensation as fully as possible. Examples include to imagine floating around the room as if caught in a hurricane or sliding along the walls around the room; rocking side to side or forward and backward as if in a rocking chair; swinging a limb back and forth or up and down, such as imagining swinging the legs up into the air and then downward through the bed, back and forth; rolling or spinning in place either back and forth or continuing in the same direction like a log in water; climbing a rope, ladder, or spiral of stairs; push-ups, playing tennis, practicing martial arts, etc. Any action or activity or sense of movement will do. Simply reimagine the *feel* of engaging in the activity as fully as possible. If possible you can physically engage in the motion or activity to cement the sensation in your memory before practice.

Mental Projection / Point-Shift

Intend, imagine, and will your awareness or perception to a location and/or time different than your physical body. A common location is right in front of your physical body, as if you're a floating field of awareness looking at your physical body, or a nonphysical specter standing before your physical body. If you imagine a physical locale you know well, or would like to visit, visualize in all the detail you can muster. Visualize it as if you were really there, walking or floating around. You can utilize pictures, or even physically visiting the place, to help your practice. Allow your experience there to be as detailed and real as you can make it.

Nonphysical Body Extrusion

Imagine a tubule of energy extruding from your solar plexus up into the air near the ceiling. This energy tube then starts to extrude energy from its tip, forming a sphere of energy which then takes the shape of your nonphysical body floating in the air. Maintaining this imagery and feeling of a nonphysical body floating in the air connected to you by a tubule of energy, move your consciousness through the tube and into the floating nonphysical body.

Relaxation

Any of the basic relaxation exercises or any combination of them can be applied. See the Relaxation basic in Chapter 8. One addition can be, when applying the Progressive Relaxation technique, to imagine pulling up consciousness from the body part as the body part is relaxed. Thus at the end of the progressive relaxation consciousness is collected into the head, and then when the head is relaxed you're allowed to float free of the physical body. This process may need to be repeated several times.

Water Temptation Technique

Allow yourself to get relatively thirsty by not drinking anything an hour or two before sleep. Place a glass of water in a convenient location, and stare at it before practice, imagining how much you want the water, how good it will taste. As you practice periodically remember the water, intending and wanting to go to it and get some water. You may have a direct projecting to the water, or you may become aware in an OBE or dream where you're trying to get water in some way.

Walk-About Simulation

Establish a route through your immediate environment, with 3 to 5 checkpoints; for instance in front of the TV, next to the refrigerator, etc. Go through the route physically a few times, remembering details of each checkpoint. What can you see from there, what can you touch from there? What do the objects you can touch feel like? What does it sound like and smell like there? Answer these questions physically, and commit observations to memory. You can even *add* objects along the route to provide definite checkpoints. Then assume your OBE Asana and *imagine* walking from checkpoint to checkpoint repeatedly, recreating the experience in detail. You may suddenly find yourself buzzing free of the physical body. You can also alternate physical and imagined walk-throughs until OBE. This is a favorite and "bread and butter" technique of author William Buhlman.

Within-Without Technique

If you will recall this is the technique I used to go to The Source. Simply go within to the core of your being in your intention, while *simultaneously* going outward with your intention as if scanning to the ends of the universe. If it helps try one and then the other, and then apply both at the same time.

CONCENTRATION TECHNIQUES

Breath Awareness

Simply focus on and be aware of your breathing, without changing it in any way.

Heartbeat Focus

Feel and hear your heartbeat, and/or the sensation of the blood pumping through your veins. You can also count the beats, intending to count for instance 100 heartbeats and then repeating at 1.

Mantra Fixative

You'll remember a *similar* exercise from the Meditation basic. For this practice it's done with more focus. Pick a phrase or word to chant repeatedly in your mind. For OBE practice it can be *anything*. It can be a lullaby or short lyric or jingle, or a spiritual word or phrase; or any group or sequence of syllables. Using mantras to OBE was a favorite technique of the Mysticweb group. The idea is to focus intently on the mantra, maintaining the single-minded intent. You can practice verbally with the mantra or jingle to start.

Mental Counting

Simply repeatedly count a predetermined range of numbers, whether counting up or counting down, for instance:

- 1 to 10
- 50 to 1
- 1 to 30
- 100 to 1
- 1 to 100
- 1 to 1000

The goal is only to focus on the numbers and the sequence. Repeat when you reach the goal number.

Remain Awake

Have the intent to remain aware and awake as you lie for sleep. Strongly intend and put effort into holding onto your wakefulness.

Sound Fixative

Play a sound that you can focus on. It can be from the radio, the TV, a lecture recording, etc. You can also mentally replay a sound or sound clip or song in your mind. The difference with this technique is that it's something you're listening to or remembering rather than something you're mentally repeating. Another sound the use is the whining sound in the ears or head.

VISUALIZATION TECHNIQUES

Activity / Movement Visualization

You can imagine yourself doing an activity – jogging, running, washing clothes, exercising, martial arts, or whatever. It can also be the visualization of a game, like a chess match. This is also a good way to remember how or to practice doing activities while practicing OBE. Visualize some manner of movement or activity. This can be driving down a hilly street, or even being shot into outer space in a large rocket. This technique focuses more on the visual aspect than the feel of the action.

Creative Visualization

Use your imagination to visualize something that holds your attention. One visualization of mine is to imagine myself engulfed in a flame, as if I'm the wick of a candle, or to imagine a flame in my third eye area. You can imagine a lion sitting starting at you, interacting with you even.

Flight Visualization

Visualize flying. If you will recall, this is my first OBE technique. You can visualize an attractive scene or environment to fly through. Include all the senses, the sight of flying through the sky or clouds, the feel and sound of air rushing by, etc.

Place-There Visualization

The imagination influences the nonphysical and can be used as an entry into the nonphysical. Visualize an imaginary place, one that you wouldn't mind visiting regularly, like your own 'fortress of solitude' in a nonphysical dimension. Design it as you will: the surrounding landscape, the make of the place, the look, the structure, etc. You can imagine usable tools, such as a chalkboard to jot down things you'll like to remember in the physical world. Visualize and imagine being there and interacting with the place. With continued practice the visualization will become more and more solid, until eventually you may find yourself actually "there." It becomes a nonphysical dimension you can actually visit through an OBE; and that others can visit as well. This is a basic practice of the Monroe Institute. This practice can also replace the Visualization and Mental Projection basic exercises as your visualization and mental projection skill develops.

Shape/Color Visualization

Visualize a shape, for instance a circle, square, cube, or cone, of a certain color. Try moving the shape around, turning it over and such, to help concentration.

WILD CARD TECHNIQUES

Combination

Try applying two or more techniques simultaneously or in succession, for instance focusing on the heartbeat *while* relaxing, or alternating relaxing and moving, or mental projection and imagined movement.

Wild Card

As you practice and learn you might develop techniques and technical variations of your own.

SEQUENCE SAMPLES

Here is the list of workable technique sequences. You can use these, build upon these, or use these as examples to build your own from the list of techniques in the previous section. *Each bullet point lists a separate projection sequence, to be used during a single practice session.* So for instance, using the first listed sequence, one could sit and do 4-2 breathing until getting alpha state phenomenon, and then lie down and continually apply progressive relaxation until completely relaxed. Then practice visualizing a shape and color until getting deep theta phenomenon, and then whenever you experience deep imagery start counting 50-1 until an OBE occurs. In each of these examples you sit during the 4-2 breathing, and then lie down after reaching alpha or theta *while sitting*, and then continue the sequence lying down. *Remember to regularly check your state to see how progressed your trance is.*

- 4-2 Rhythmic Breathing; Progressive Relaxation; Shape/Color Visualization; 50-1 Countdown

- 4-2 Rhythmic Breathing; Relaxation

- 4-2 Rhythmic Breathing; 50-1 Countdown; Imagined Movement – imagining *rolling* or *spinning* in place like a log in water

- 4-2 Rhythmic Breathing; Relax-Move Technique (alternate between deeply relaxing for a few minutes and then physically moving to a different position or asana)

- 4-2 Rhythmic Breathing; Mantra Fixative

- 4-2 Rhythmic Breathing; Point Shift and Imagined Movement *climbing a ladder* combo (alternate between a shifted position and imagining the feel of climbing a ladder)

- 4-2 Rhythmic Breathing; Place-There Visualization

- 4-2 Rhythmic Breathing; Slow Down

- 4-2 Rhythmic Breathing; Mind Blank

- 4-2 Rhythmic Breathing; Energy Working; Shape/Color Visualization; Displacement

- 4-2 Rhythmic Breathing; Flight Visualization

- 4-2 Rhythmic Breathing; Arm-Up and Relaxation and Sleep Signal Focus combo (keep an arm balanced up at the forearm, and continue to relax into sleep)

- 4-2 Rhythmic Breathing; Imagined Movement imagining sliding around the room along the walls; Shape/Color Visualization

- 4-2 Rhythmic Breathing; Triple Spheres Relaxation; Nonphysical Body Extrusion, repeating until OBE

FINISHING THE SHIFT

There are several ways to finish the shift into an OBE if it doesn't happen automatically. Often you'll simply find yourself floating, or in a different location, depending upon what technique you use, and depending on if you lose awareness or not during the practice. For instance with Nonphysical Body Extrusion you can suddenly find yourself floating at the ceiling.

There are various ways the experience of spontaneously exiting the physical body can take. In one experience I became aware spinning up into the air like a helicopter blade, as if lying on my back atop a spinning disc, pausing stationary at the ceiling. This can happen with techniques that focus less on movement, such as Basic Relaxation. With Relax-Move you will likely find yourself paralyzed and needing to manually move from the physical body. In that case you would relax and then move away from the physical body just as you would move physically. *Don't move physically*, but relax and move *as if* moving physically. If you were in fact in pre-OBE paralysis the movement will in fact be nonphysical. If you suddenly find yourself in a different location simply explore from there, or intend or fly to where you'd rather be. This often happens when we lose awareness mid practice.

Sometimes nonphysical movement can be mistaken for physical movement, as the nonphysical body can feel just like the physical one. Especially early on, the slow and labored nature of initial nonphysical movement just as the experience begins will signify the movement is nonphysical. Just continue to walk or crawl away from the physical body until you can move freely, or intend yourself to a different location. If you intend a destination you can experience flying there at enormous speeds, teleporting there, or lose awareness and find yourself there.

Anytime you recognize that you are in deep theta or delta you can try to relax and move away. Relax, let go, and sit up, roll to the side, or what have you. If you happen to move physically you can just go back to the practice. It's no big deal, and it will happen. But if you don't try moving you may miss an opportunity to experience. If you consistently find yourself moving physically that means you need to allow yourself into a deeper altered state before trying. Also when in deep theta or delta you can try willing or intending yourself up or away from the physical body, or to a particular destination. One time I simply willed and intended to float into the air and experienced full body vibrations, and just floated out of the body and glided over into the upper corner of the room. Try both manually moving and intending and see which works better for you.

If you see a deep void you may likely have spontaneously projected into the nonphysical. Intend or will yourself to a destination of your choice. If you seem to be in a virtual reality movie or lucid dream (immersive imagery), in the same way as before relax and move into the out-of-body experience. In a lucid dream I suggest feeling for your physical body first, which will clear away the dream imagery but still have you in delta or perhaps aroused a bit into mid or deep theta, but still ready to relax and move away from the physical body. If you experience yourself in the middle of very strong full-body vibrations try sitting up or pushing off so that you float into the air, or any other manner of movement. You can also apply the Vibration Strobe technique which can have you simply float free. A good tactic as well, especially if you are finding it difficult to move, is to wiggle or minutely move into the experience. Relax and twist nonphysically to the side a bit. Then relax more and twist the other way. Go back and forth in larger and larger increments until you can roll free of the physical body. If the OBE ends quickly you can continue the exercise you were doing and try again. It's possible to initiate OBEs many times in succession. As you practice you'll be able to extend extrusions for longer and longer. Don't be surprised if early on you get so excited that you inadvertently end the experience after a few seconds. Extreme excitement or fear while in the nonphysical state can trigger "fail-safe" which causes you to catapult back to or get pulled back into the physical body.

You may notice spontaneous movement such as an arm floating, or that you're suddenly in a different position than you were physically. Simply go with the movement – let your nonphysical body follow the arm as you roll out, for instance. Or simply get up from your new position and explore. If you use a movement technique the movement you imagine may initiate the experience. So for instance if you imagine spinning like a log in water you may suddenly find that you *are* suddenly *actually* spinning in this way – which can be *very* disconcerting, so try to be prepared for this. You can then push off into the air or what have you. Or if you imagine repeatedly swinging your legs up into the air and then through the bed, you may suddenly realize that you had lost awareness but that you now feel your legs sinking *through* the bed. You can starting crawling through the air away from your physical body.

You can continue practicing the last technique in the sequence until you are "out" or you fall asleep. It's okay to stop the session short as well, especially if you experience very uncomfortable altered state phenomenon or are getting extremely sleepy. That may be a good time to get "sleep comfortable" and practice going into the Sleep Signal. You will likely experience getting extremely sleepy as you practice, which is understandable. Eventually you'll be able to stay conscious apart from the feeling of sleep, allowing your physical body to sleep as you remain aware. As you continue to practice the experience of feeling like you're sleepy will decrease, yet you'll still progress through the same states, as your ability to remain consciously aware in these states will solidify. One issue with the experience of extreme sleepiness is the tendency to just turn over and go to sleep. Regular concentration practice will help overcome this tendency.

PROGRESSION FLOW CHARTS

Here is a collection of flow charts to further provide examples of how the process may go in your practices. *The left side of the flow charts list techniques in the sequence. The right side of the flow chart shows common state marker phenomenon that may occur while using that particular technique. In bold I'll list how you can finish the shift at that point if you'd like to do so.*

In all practice sessions you can either focus on the state marker phenomena you experience to deepen your state, *or* continue with the technique you were applying to continue into deeper altered states. If you focus on the state marker phenomenon remember to keep a light or gentle focus to not disrupt your state. However far you get in any session acknowledge it, and seek to get as far or perhaps just a little bit further next time. If you follow my advice to make a goal of progressive state plateaus you would practice at finishing the shift only after regularly hitting at least full theta for a week or two.

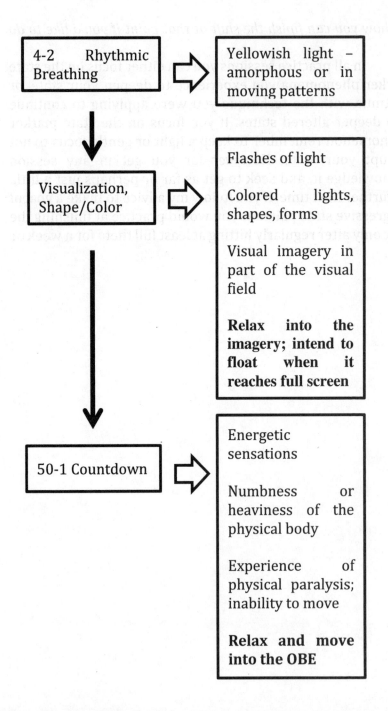

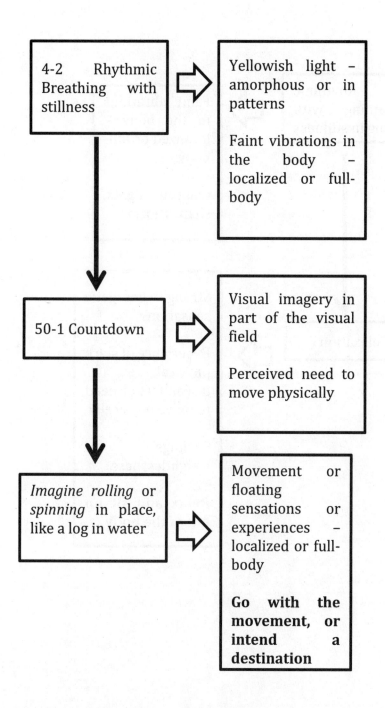

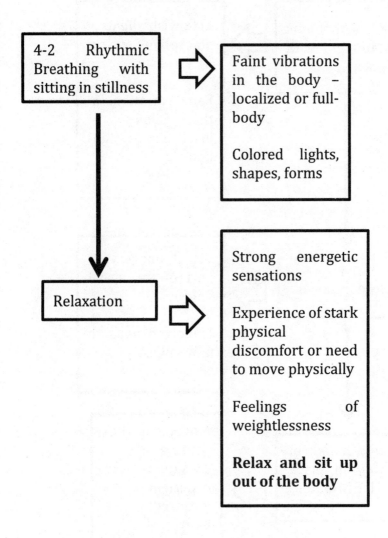

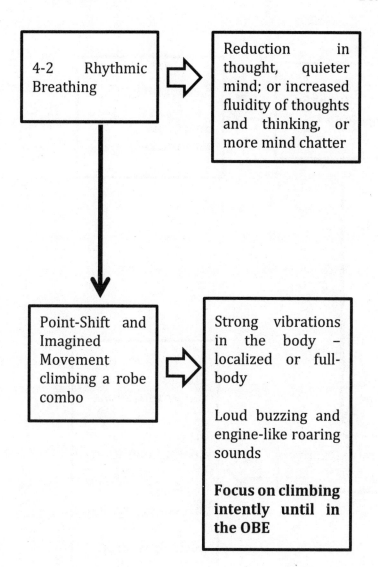

4-2 Rhythmic Breathing

Reduction in thought, quieter mind; or increased fluidity of thoughts and thinking, or more mind chatter

Point-Shift and Imagined Movement climbing a robe combo

Strong vibrations in the body – localized or full-body

Loud buzzing and engine-like roaring sounds

Focus on climbing intently until in the OBE

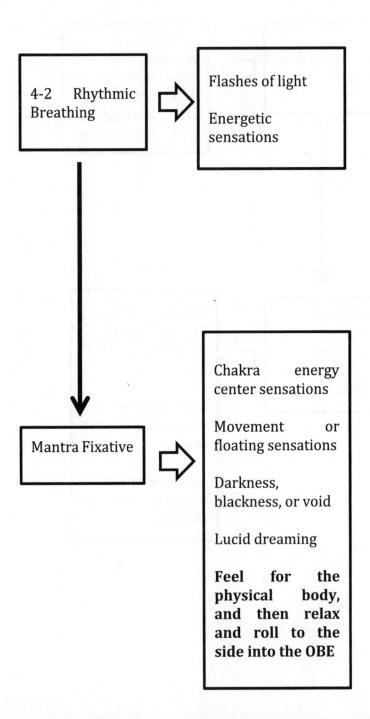

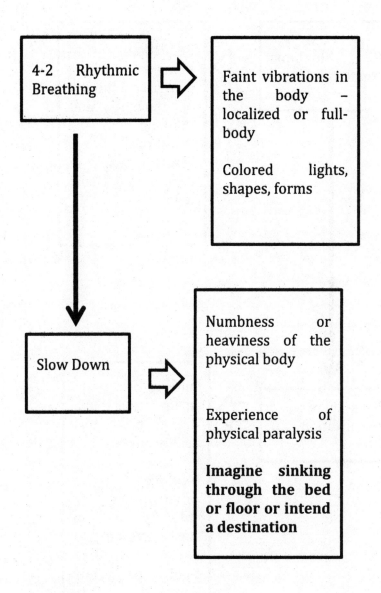

4-2   Rhythmic Breathing

Faint vibrations in the body – localized or full-body

Colored lights, shapes, forms

Slow Down

Numbness or heaviness of the physical body

Experience of physical paralysis

Imagine sinking through the bed or floor or intend a destination

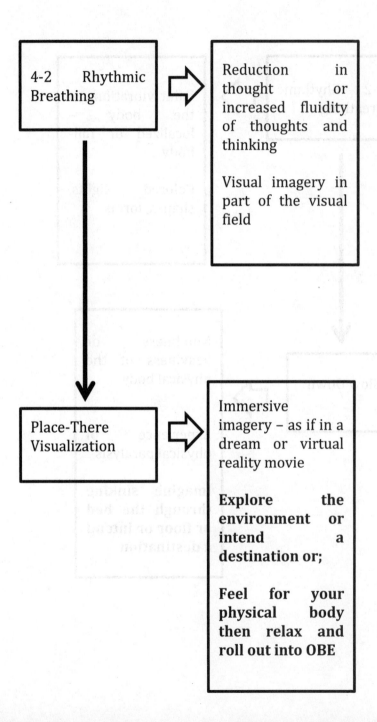

4-2 Rhythmic Breathing

Reduction in thought or increased fluidity of thoughts and thinking

Visual imagery in part of the visual field

Place-There Visualization

Immersive imagery – as if in a dream or virtual reality movie

Explore the environment or intend a destination or;

Feel for your physical body then relax and roll out into OBE

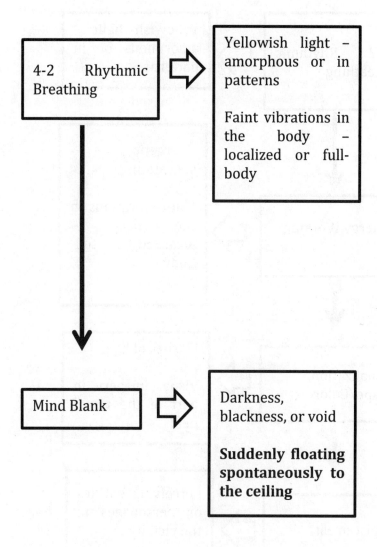

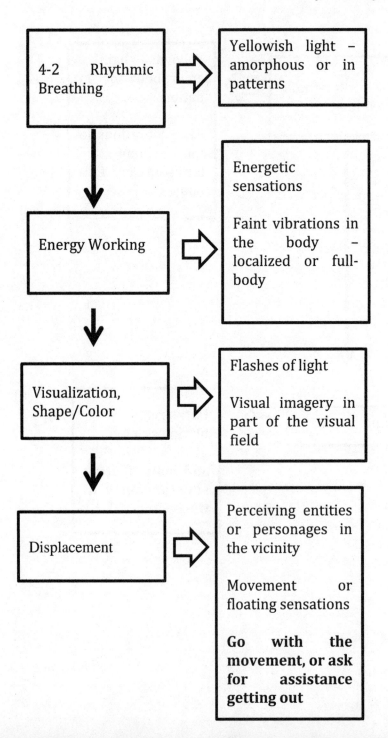

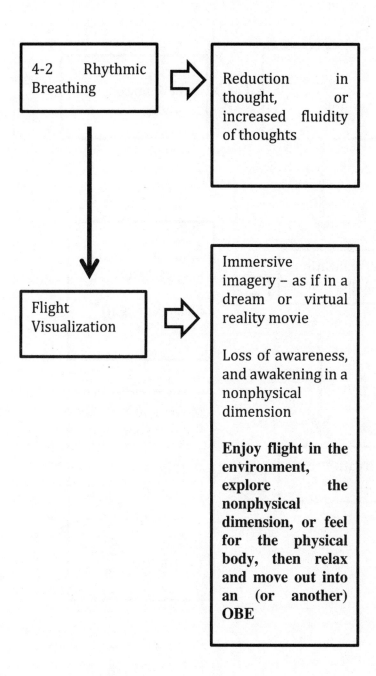

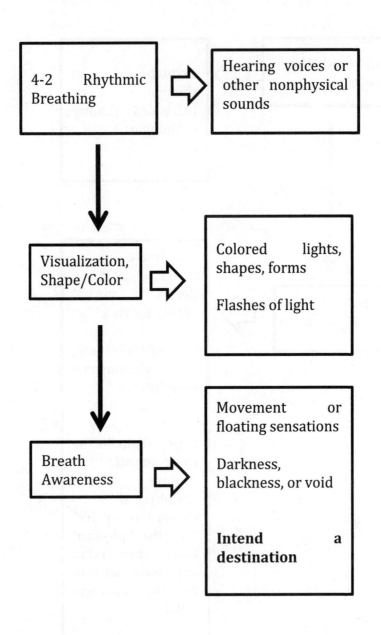

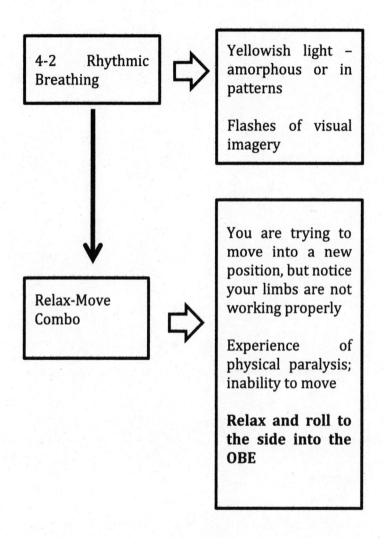

4-2 Rhythmic Breathing

→ Yellowish light – amorphous or in patterns

Flashes of visual imagery

Relax-Move Combo

→ You are trying to move into a new position, but notice your limbs are not working properly

Experience of physical paralysis; inability to move

Relax and roll to the side into the OBE

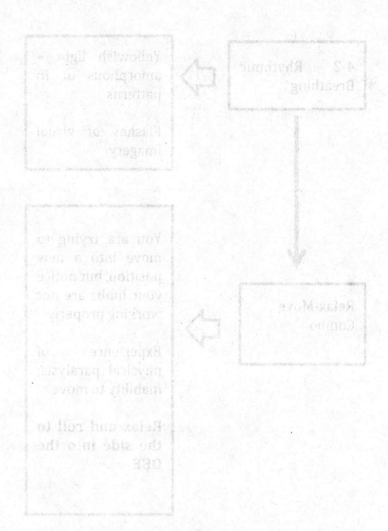

11 – DREAMING AND THE OBE

THE UNIVERSAL DREAM

The entire world, the entire universe, is a dream. Within it are various forms of dreams which we demarcate into "real" and "unreal," "reality" and "dream," according to our experiences and perceptions.[31] It would be more accurate to call our waking physical life diurnal dreams and the worlds we experience while our physical body is sleeping nocturnal dreams – in truth physical life is just a state of mind or consciousness, just like the out-of-body state.[32]

NOCTURNAL DREAMS

That being said, from our usual perspective in Earth third density societies we designate the physical world as real, and the worlds we perceive while our physical body is sleeping as unreal. But even reverie that we seemingly experience only in our personal mind is made of nonphysical matter or thought, and if held and reinforced by repeated visualization influences nonphysical matter in the larger nonphysical world, which can be perceived by others. These become stable constructs and can be journeyed to through an OBE. *What we normally call "dreams" can be defined as temporary and localized nonphysical constructs made subconsciously or unconsciously while the physical body is sleeping.* These are our personal nocturnal dreams. These are

---

[31] See non-dualistic thought systems such as *A Course in Miracles* and the Indian Vedanta.

[32] Diurnal – happening during the day; nocturnal – happening during the night.

our individual reveries in our minds as we sleep. Through these reverie experiences we act out traumas, desires, fears, and etcetera. That we usually unconsciously or subconsciously make nocturnal dreams lends them to psychoanalysis and self-introspection. We can know what is in our minds by what we are projecting.

Nocturnal dreams also serve to keep us asleep, as we get caught up in the occurrences of the nocturnal dream and thus embed ourselves in sleep to continue the dream. I'm sure we have all had the experience of waking up later than desired due to infatuation with the happenings of a dream. Another occurrence is taking the sound of an alarm in the physical world, making a dream representation of the sound – for instance a tornado siren, and then continuing with the dream. What we normally call nocturnal dreams are imaginings in the same way that our daydreams are when we have lapses of attention in the physical world. But since the physical body is asleep we're free to fully engage ourselves in these self-created worlds. When we enter the deep theta or delta ranges of brain wave activity our reveries are experienced as virtual reality worlds. When we become conscious in these reverie words we call it *lucid dreaming.* In these instances the brain is in the delta state and the nonphysical body proper is usually disengaged or undocked from but hovering near the physical body.

Nocturnal dream imagery can correlate with the OBE state, for instance you may dream of going up on an airplane, and this coincides with nonphysically floating up to the ceiling as you hit deep delta during sleep. And you may then dream of going down in an elevator, and *feel* the descent – the *actual* descent being your nonphysical descent back into the physical body from the ceiling. Often vertical movement in a nocturnal dream, especially when there is a sensation of motion, coincides with movement in the out-of-body state. So then often the nocturnal dreams we have, we dream up while unconsciously out-of-body. When through your altered state practices you start to become more conscious during sleep, and you sense movement and open your awareness, you may notice that you're floating around the room nonphysically as you were dreaming of flying in an airplane for instance.

UNCLEAR OBES MISTAKEN AS DREAMS

Another aspect of "dreams" is that we can be in the out-of-body state proper but *mistake* the OBE to be a nocturnal dream. An OBE experienced through cloudy awareness can be unclear and seem less "real," and be easily mistaken for a conventional nocturnal reverie-type dream. [33] Recall my experience meeting Louis through OBE. Due to accumulated experience I knew it was an OBE. If not for my experience I could have mistaken it for a dream. And of course there was the unprompted verification from Louis' side of the experience as further confirmation. I am sure that many so-called "dreams" are half remembered, or cloudily perceived, OBEs. And as you travel you'll no doubt see friends and relatives having out-of-body experiences but when you tell them about it the next day they'll often have no memory of it, but will sometimes remember "dreaming" about you.

HYBRID OBE/DREAM EXPERIENCES

To complicate the matter, sometimes dream *and* non-dream elements can be interwoven. I read in *Preparing for Contact*[34] of a lady who dreamt of receiving contact from ETs through her dream computer. Messages would come through

---

[33] Remember that practices of concentration and visualization can be used to help clear this up; and of course sometimes we just have unclear OBEs.

[34] By Lyssa Royal.

on the screen that she could read. The messages turned out to be real telepathic messages from an actual physical world ET communicating telepathically with her while she slept. She received the physical world telepathic messages and incorporated them into her dream. This is similar to how a physical clock alarm becomes a siren within the dream. Perhaps if she had skill in state acquisition, and had made progress in pushing her awareness threshold back, this telepathic contact would have been *conscious* and deliberate, in full awareness of what was actually going on. One example is my *Beings of Light* experiences. Perhaps sometimes when people wake up with brilliant ideas they actually received communication during sleep but don't remember it. Recall that both David Adair and Stephen Hawking received information and formulas through dreams.

LEVELS OF NOCTURNAL DREAMS

Kurt Leland shares in his book *Otherwhere* a gradation metric for levels of wakefulness during nocturnal dreams. Ironically such a gradation can be made for the overall universal dream, with minds absolutely immersed in their physical identity with no awareness of anything beyond at Level Zero, and minds so fully conscious and aware that they are actually beyond the dream at Level Ten, for instance the level of enlightened masters such as Y'shua, The Great Sun, or Byron Katie. [35] Here is the nocturnal dream gradation as shared in *Otherwhere*, augmented with a few findings of my own:

- Level Zero – no recall of dreams or even that you had dreams

---

[35] See *The Disappearance of the Universe* for the first two, and www.thework.com for the third.

- Level One – recall that one has dreamt without remembering any details of what was dreamt
- Level Two – recall of disjointed fragments of dreams, or isolated images and feelings from the dream
- Level Three – the experience of watching oneself in the dream rather than participating in it
- Level Four – full participation in the action of the dream
- Level Five – long and involved dream plots; dream continuity from previous dreams
- Level Six – very vivid colors and sounds, detail begins emerging in dream recall
- Level Seven – the presence of textures, smells, and tastes in the dream
- Level Eight – the ability to think rationally, and actively use mental processes
- Level Nine – *active dreaming* – at-will rational application of supernormal powers in the dream, such as flying or environment alteration
- Level Ten – *lucid dreaming* – one is fully conscious in the dream state and fully aware that one is dreaming

REMEMBERING NOCTURNAL DREAMS

Simply practicing state acquisition regularly and journaling consistently develops the ability to remember dreams. Yet there are things that can accelerate this process. A *dream journal* can help dream recall, *and* heighten dream lucidity by heightening awareness during the dream in preparation to journal; the greater the detail of your dream journals the greater the reciprocal effect of heightened awareness during dreams. Making note of the level of dream experienced per the aforementioned gradation metric can add another facet to a dream journal. The heightened awareness and recall developed from dream journaling helps OBE techniques and OBE practices by helping to increase general lucidity. A handwritten, typed, or voice recorded dream journal will do; whatever recording method or media. If for whatever reason you don't actually journal your dreams a detailed mental review of what you dreamt may suffice.

If you have difficulty remembering your dreams try following any thought snippets of the dream you can remember. If you remember driving down a street in a dream, focus on that. Consider it. Picture it. Driving where? Driving... driving... driving how? Driving... driving... was I with someone? Driving... driving... Close your eyes and try to reimagine the scene, and see if you can fill out the scene as you make a trail of thought that ignites your memory. This process helps with remembering anything actually, such as lyrics to a song you are to trying to remember, or names of people. The more you practice remembering and journaling your dreams, and the more diligently and detailed you do so, the better and better will your dream recall and consequently your general lucidity become. You'll soon find that you have an entire sleep life going on that you've scarcely been aware of!

BECOMING LUCID IN DREAMS

Lucid dreaming is the experience of becoming fully aware during regular nocturnal dream reverie. The benefit of developing this skill in relation to OBE is that lucid dreams can be used as launch pads for OBEs. Becoming lucid in a dream is *almost* the equivalent of going consciously into delta through state acquisition. I say almost because with lucid dreams there will by nature be a clouded perception, subconscious projection, etc. But all the same you can practice either state acquisition or lucid dreaming to enter the OBE state, or you can practice both, with lucid dreaming being the backup plan in case you fall asleep during state acquisition. And you can use the idea of focusing on and reconnecting with your physical body and then reinitiating the OBE to clear any subconscious projections or lack of clarity.

Two simple practices can greatly help increase your ability to lucidly dream. The first is the practice of *awareness*, which was covered in Chapter 8. Heavy focus on the practice of awareness will greatly increase your experience of lucid dreaming. To embolden this practice you can add *awareness checking.* Awareness checking is the practice of actually checking whether you are physically awake or physically asleep. Remember, in normal nocturnal dreams we aren't aware that we are dreaming. So if you're new to all this, *this* could be a nocturnal dream and you not even know it... so, are you dreaming now? You can for instance take a little jump into the air, and see if you can float or fly. You can pull your finger and see if it will stretch like a rubber band. You can check your environment and see if it adds up to your normal waking life: What time is it? Are you where you would normally be at this time? Is your environment as it should be? Etc. Establish a minimum number of awareness exercises per day, for instance 10 little jumps, 10 finger pulls, 1 awareness walk, and 10 general awareness checks each day.

And remember the common occurrence of masking vertical OBE movement in dream reverie. *Whenever* you seem to be going through a vertical movement process, for instance up or down in an elevator, up or down stairs, up or down in an airplane, even up or down on a bumpy road in a car drive, this is a great time to do a very involved awareness check (as soon as it's safe to do so if driving). Of course if you're in an elevator with people at work it may not be practical to take a little jump. If driving you may not want to take your hands off of the steering wheel to pull your finger. But do what you can. Observe whether the elevator is working properly. Notice the time and if it's reasonable to be in the elevator then. Notice whether the street you're driving on is an actual street.

I once had a dream where an escalator was not working properly. Rather than a gentle slope like stairs it went vertically straight down! I had to hold onto the railings to not fall as I went vertically straight down on the malfunctioning or very poorly designed escalator! This was clearly imagery masking the vertical descent of my out-of-body self. If you're at work, is it time for you to be at work? How did you get to work? *Really investigating* these questions will make a habit that carries over into nocturnal dreams, and you'll start to catch yourself dreaming more and more frequently.

And secondly and lastly is the aforementioned practice of the *dream journal*. Keep an *extremely detailed* and consistent dream journal. Note where you were, what you did. Consider if this is a place or time or person or event you've dreamt of before. How long did the dream seem in dream time? Did it seem to be a message or indication of a belief you subconsciously hold? Could it have been a hazily aware OBE? Did you have movement sensations at any point during the dream? *Really* flesh out your dream journal. You may find recurring points that can help you become lucid.

USING LDS AS OBE LAUNCHPAD

With consistent awareness practices and dream journaling you will at some point become aware during a nocturnal dream. Upon becoming aware simply feel for your physical body, and upon becoming aware of your body relax and roll to the side, or any other form of movement into the out-of body-experience; or intend to be at your intended destination. It's no different than if you entered deep theta or delta through state acquisition.

Note that I say feel for your physical body because that's how it feels. But in fact the body you first encounter when returning from a lucid dream or deep altered state reverie is actually the *nonphysical* body. Likely the nonphysical body is hovering close to the physical body, with your mind stuck in reverie. You then proceed to initiate the conscious out-of-body experience just as if you had reached deep theta or delta through meditation techniques. The deep altered state is the same, except there was some lack of awareness and some unconscious projections thrown in the mix.

If the "dream" was actually a true OBE that you were hazily aware in, the process works the same. You feel for your body to reset and clear away the cobwebs, and then re-initiate the experience.

DREAM CONVERGENCE

Another way to start a lucid dream is to consciously intend oneself directly into a dream. With dream convergence you *imagine and intend to reenter a dream you've just woken from.* The effectiveness of this technique can be fantastic. In a sense you use recent dream locales as bases for shifting quickly and seamlessly into a deep altered state. And the technique can also be used to reenter nonphysical realms. This is the technique I used in the experience entitled "Demonology," when I went back to fight the two nonphysical entities that bested me. If you have had a vivid dream you can imagine and recall the scene as you go back to sleep, intending and willing yourself back. It is not necessary that it be a dream you have just woken from. It can be a dream you had in the past, but most effective is a dream you've just woken from. You may suddenly find yourself standing in the dream location – or you may find it's not actually a "dream location" at all, but a nonphysical dimension. If it turns out to be a dream or you are unsure simply feel for your body, then relax and move into an OBE as usual.

12 – OBE MOVEMENT

INITIAL MOVEMENT

At the beginning of OBE ability, as well as *potentially* at the start of *any* OBE, you may experience difficulty moving. It can be likened to being suspended in molasses or some thick heavier-than-water substance that makes it very difficult to move. With continued practice – especially basics practice to develop – movement becomes easier. If you have difficulty moving you can try relaxing to help you move easier, or to simply will and intend yourself to a different location. Another good tactic is to crawl away from the physical body. Just *keep crawling* until you can move freely. It may help to close your nonphysical visual perceptions as you crawl – the intention is like you are closing your physical eyes.

MODES OF MOVEMENT

After you are in the OBE state you can move in a variety of ways. Four basic modes of movement include *locomotion*, *flight*, *teleportation*, and *stretch-method*.

Locomotion refers to the process of moving about as if in a physical body in contact with a surface, for instance crawling or walking or running about. This is a good way to move as you become familiar with the experience. The experience is just as if you're moving with the physical body. One thing about locomotion is, sometimes when passing through windows, walls, or doors there's a tendency to shift to other dimensions. If this happens for you try teleportation to get to a distant physical universe locale.

Flight can occur at various speeds, from barely moving to many times the speed of light – like warp speed on the TV series *Star Trek*. You can take off and fly around just as if you would if you had super powers and could fly physically. Intend and will yourself in the direction and at the speed you want to go and you'll move as intended. If you have trouble with this you can try swimming through the air, as if you're in a pool of water.

Teleportation is simply a matter of willing or intending where you want to be. You can thus appear there in an instant. As stated this process can be used as a way to initiate the out-of-body experience itself, intending where one wants to be as one goes to sleep, or upon reaching the theta-delta level of altered state. One potential complication with teleportation early on is that a lack of focus during the OBE can cause one to teleport haphazardly. I have had experiences where several times throughout I was suddenly at a different location. Teleportation also takes the form of simply becoming aware already at an intended or desired destination after having fallen asleep or lost awareness during practice. Conversely with intending or willing a destination you can rapidly move to the destination via flight.

With the *Stretch Method* you can imagine or intend to stretch to the destination you want to reach, "stretching" your awareness or intent as if reaching out with your arms while your feet stay planted where they are. Upon stretching your hands to where you want to be you complete the move by letting go of your previous location and resolving yourself at the new locale. This was a favorite of Robert Monroe's.

13 – SCHEDULE AND RITUALS

STANDARD PRACTICE SCHEDULE

One of the greatest helps to basics progress and OBE success is having a regular schedule of practice. By simply practicing at the same time every day you develop a very potent momentum that begins to carry you along toward success. At a particular time every day or night you can become *attuned* to and *magnetized* for entering meditation, a heightened state of concentration, or the out-of-body state. It's like how after years of waking up at a certain time we start to wake up a minute or two before the alarm sounds, and no longer need the alarm.

Determine what times and what days are the things you must do, and around those times schedule your practices so that you can practice regularly without interference. Once established only your will to do or lack thereof can interfere with successful maintenance of your schedule. If you make a checklist for practices you can include time(s) of practice on the checklist by each exercise.

ESTABLISHING A RITUAL

A ritual is simply a series of actions that you habitually perform in the same way. Just like having a regular practice schedule, having a regular sequence of techniques that you use in your practices can greatly help your progress. You can develop the same mental, energetic, and physical habit that having a regular schedule develops. For instance you could always start your practice with the 4-2 rhythmic breathing meditation. Thus this meditation will begin to signal an entry into altered states. Ritual can also include finding a sequence of exercise you like and always using that same sequence. Another ritual could be to always start your practice session sitting, and after the same number of minutes of sitting practice lie down to continue your practice session. And rituals can become more and more elaborate, such as lighting incense at a certain point in your session. Rituals can also include things you do *around* the practice session, such as playing a particular piece of music. I suggest developing a ritual, as simple or as elaborate as you like, but develop something that becomes a staple of your OBE practices.

SHEDDING SCHEDULE AND RITUAL

And remember to keep it in perspective. Developing a schedule and ritual is *not* a matter of superstition but a matter of psychological habit, which can accelerate success, much like physical repetitions and drills in sports. But to help make sure you don't grow dependent upon your schedules and rituals, and to help develop a more free flowing ability to enter heightened (focused beta) and altered (alpha, theta, and delta) states, I suggest letting schedule and ritual go when you start to have regular success. When you can OBE regularly at your regularly scheduled time, with your habitual ritualistic elements, try practicing earlier or later. Try practicing at the total *opposite* time of day. Try leaving off something of your ritual – skip the incense for a try, for instance. Start with something small, until you've completely shed the schedule and ritual. Then you'll be able to OBE any time, any place, and under any circumstance. And varying times and places of practice can yield nonphysical observations that you may not have come across otherwise, for instance perhaps practicing at a different time allows you to nonphysically observe a local environmental phenomenon that happens only at that time.

14 – TROUBLESHOOTING

MEDICATIONS AND LACK OF FOCUS

Medications and other things that cause you to quickly fall asleep or keep you from getting to sleep can be overcome. I have heard of people experiencing a negative effect with various chemicals including prescription drugs like Ritalin, or alcohol, or marijuana; like less ability to remember dreams or less ability to enter or remain in deep sleep. But I'm sure with practice any negative effect can be overcome. In the end it's all just a function of mind and consciousness, and at advanced skill levels you'll learn that you can just direct yourself to where you want to experience being.

If you need to take a medication that causes you to fall asleep quickly you can try focusing more strongly to help yourself remain aware. Frequent practicing of the Concentration and Awareness basics will help with this. If you take a medication that makes it difficult for you to fall asleep or remain asleep you can use a technique that requires strong focus, such as one of the concentration techniques. If you concentrate strongly enough you can push entry into altered states. Or you can focus on relaxation and meditation to counter the drug's effects.

LOSING AWARENESS

Losing awareness is a common and natural part of progression at state acquisition and OBE skill. As you practice, accept your progresses. Flashes of light and then losing consciousness is actually good progress if you normally just fall into a dark oblivion when you sleep. You've reached an altered state, and with continued practice your conscious awareness will progress further and further into the sleep state. As discussed, concentration and awareness practice will help with this, as well as meditation practice. It's a matter of training yourself to remain aware during deeper states, through patient regular practice, which develops flexibility of consciousness.

TERROR OF THE THRESHOLD, ET AL

You may want to check the apartment, house, and/or room before you go to sleep or practice, so you can be certain no one is in the home that shouldn't be there, and no one can get in who shouldn't enter. I say this because it's common to perceive someone or something else in the room as you go into an OBE, which can be either an actual entity or a projection of your own mind. Knowing the home is secure can help overcome a knee-jerk reaction – thinking an intruder is physically in the room.

The experience of an entity being there at the onset of an OBE – when perceived as frightening – has been called the "Terror of the Threshold." Some report this specter as being a gruesome-looking monster. Some call it a test of the would-be OBE explorer. If you will recall, my "Terror of the Threshold" was the Freddy Krueger entity. Eventually I defeated him, and was then free to explore the nonphysical unhindered.

In the nonphysical realms your thoughts and intentions are just as physical as physical objects in the physical world. If you experience being attacked you can use your imagination in various ways to defend yourself. I've imagined a sword to use as a weapon; I've imagined an army of people to swarm my would-be attacker. These have both worked successfully. And of course you can use your hands and feet and manually beat an entity up. In the end I think it doesn't matter – like a high school bully if you just stand up for yourself, and know within that you're safe, negative nonphysical entities will simply leave you alone. Another tactic to avoid any conflict is to simply *fly up*. If you're in a nonphysical realm and you fly upward you'll enter progressively more light and vibrant realms that negative entities won't be able to follow you through.

My "Freddy" experience I think is an extreme example. Usually what you'll perceive in your nonphysical environment as you exit the body is just another entity in the room. Other time it's usually a good-natured being. You may think it is a physical intruder that you try to get up to do something about – *only to realize that you're paralyzed and can't move*. You can remember and affirm your pre-OBE state and relax and move into an OBE. Or you can try to physically move to address the potential intruder. To help reinitiate physical movement wiggle a single body part, like a pinkie finger. If you find it was a projection or a nonphysical entity you can relax back into trance and re-initiate the OBE to meet your guest; your reintegration will likely dispel any projections. Minor "terrors" can arise as well, for instance my experience of a cat nibbling my fingers. If you know they're nonphysical you can ignore them. If you fear they're physical the same process applies – reintegrate, check it out, and reinitiate practice if all is clear.

Psychic Protection

Some speak of a need to protect oneself by various means when practicing the out-of-body experience. Various reasons may be given, such as negative energies around you, or even fear of being possessed. I don't see either of these things as a concern. In my experience it's simply impossible for any other entity to forcibly take over our physical bodies while we're "out." They just don't have that power. I have heard of an instance of two of people *consensually switching bodies* for a while, though. If you have a concern about negative psychic occurrences, something that helped me early on was to visualize or imagine myself surrounded or enveloped in a shield of *brilliant* sparkling light. Intend and know that this shield will protect your body and keep it safe from nonphysical intruders while you travel. Such a shield can be so powerful as to keep even well-wishing nonphysical entities away. To accentuate this you can interlock your fingers in the aforementioned Interlocking Ring Mudra[36] as you visualize. Simply do this every time before you do any OBE practices, intending, visualizing, and feeling the shield, its radiance, strength, security, and protection, and know that you are safe.

THE PSYCHOLOGICAL BARRIER

There is a psychological barrier that may play a central role in the failure to achieve the OBE. The basis of this barrier can be different for everyone, and can be a combination of things. It could be based upon fear of the experience. It could be based upon fear of dying through the experience. It could be based upon fear of the unknown, and could even take the form of internally filtering or screening what we perceive or recall. It could be based upon fear of being strange or weird by engaging in these activities. And it could even be based upon various degrees of fear of success (or fear of failure), or a sense of unworthiness, which would likely be affecting other areas of life as well. I've taught people to OBE before, and told them the proper technique to do given what they were experiencing, and so many times they would simply not practice what I'd instruct. Either they simply wouldn't practice

---

[36] Chapter 8, in the Energy Working section.

at all, or they would practice something they picked up from some other source that happened to be less efficient. And they would experience failure and then give up. I've also experienced doing the same thing at various points in my overall journey – for instance the immediate projection techniques Louis taught me but in the end were just too jarring for me. Fear of success or failure can also take various forms of delay: avoiding OBE practice, skipping basics practices, etc.; in order to avoid succeeding or failing by not trying at all – but that's the only sure way to *ensure* you never succeed.

You may not succeed immediately, but if you put forth the time and effort with the techniques and methods herein *you will* succeed. If you find yourself delaying a lot, or your progress seems slow, one exercise is to question yourself. Look within and investigate if you do have any fears. Just bringing them to light can lessen their affect upon you.

- Fear of the experience – there's nothing to be afraid of. You OBE regularly but are unconscious of it.
- Fear of injury or death – I had this when I realized what was going on. I eventually decided to go through with it anyway. I've found this fear unfounded.
- Fear of the unknown – this one's a kicker. You'll no doubt learn things that you didn't previously know. That's nothing to fear, just an adventure to enjoy.
- Fear of being strange or weird – the cutting edge of progress is *always* seen as crazy, strange, or weird by the status quo. You can be an ambassador to a new age of Human existence; embrace it.
- Fear of success (or fear of failure) – fear of success is likely due to one of the aforementioned points. Fear of failure is unfounded – I've taught dozens of people, and by the time you read this maybe hundreds or thousands of people, to their first out-of-body

experiences, with these techniques and methodologies. Apply yourself and you'll succeed.

- Sense of unworthiness – this can be a big one. An easy solution may be to refer back to the fact that you OBE regularly anyway each time you hit delta during sleep. So you must be worthy by natural right.

- Fear of religious conflict – For those who are religious, given that it's a natural part of our makeup, OBE can't be against any creator God. There can even be a case made that it's referenced in the Bible: there's reference to a "silver cord" breaking at death (Ecclesiastes 12:6) and of John being called up to heaven and suddenly being "in the spirit" and then in heaven (Revelation 4:2).

THE IMAGERY TRAP

The imagery trap is an important concept for the traveler to be aware of. It's when you think you are experiencing the out-of-body state but perceive instead a vivid nocturnal dream. The out-of-body experience proper is in fact going on with the nonphysical body hovering close to the physical body, while you are engaging the imagined environment *believing* it's an OBE. Imagery traps may also take the form of people and entities that we project into our nonphysical environment. If you are unsure if you're in a true OBE, or whether what you're seeing is objective, reintegrate and then reinitiate the experience. This resets the experience and clears out any unconscious projections. Try using intent and will to clear your perceptions. Try getting more distance from the body. You can even mentally yell "Clarity Now!" If nothing works, or movement seems strange, or your perceptions are irreparably dreamy, hazy, or unclear, resetting is good to do.

15 – THE OBE ENVIRONMENT

THE NONPHYSICAL BODY

Recall my early experience entitled *Multiple Bodied We*, in which I suddenly became aware hovering in the upper corner of my bedroom and observed my triumvirate state of consciousness, nonphysical body, and physical body. This demonstrates the two basic ways of nonphysical travel, in a physical-like energy body, and as disembodied consciousness.

The nonphysical body can be experienced along a spectrum of seeming solidity. Sometimes it seems very ghostly or ephemeral, as if not even there. I remember one time sitting in a chair practicing altered states and feeling a nonphysical arm float free. I was able to move it around and it felt very light and extremely skinny and delicate. Sometimes the nonphysical body can seem quite physical, just like the physical body. It seems most solid immediately after a manual exit from the physical body, such as rolling to the side or sitting up. Sometimes you can reach the appropriate state and disengage from the physical body and not even realize it because the nonphysical body can feel so physical. Another indication of how physical the nonphysical can feel is that you can actually have sex in the nonphysical. Sometimes those kinds of "dreams" we have aren't nocturnal dreams at all. The experience of being a point or field of consciousness is like being a bodiless roaming eye. I've read that as consciousness one can visually perceive 360 degrees around, though I've only had visual perception to where I directed my intention just like physical sight.

Other than potentially the experience entitled *Astral Cord Experience, Maybe* I do not have any perceptions of an astral cord. The astral cord is supposed to be a nonphysical link between the physical body and the nonphysical body. I've never really liked the idea, as the idea seems limiting to me. I would like to think of any connection between the physical body and the traveling consciousness as a wave-type phenomenon, more like an infinitely ranged wireless phone and its base receiver. Perhaps "the cord" represents a formless link, given form according to the thinking at the time, as I'm doing with the wireless phone analogy.

DISTANCE AND SPEED CAPABILITIES

I am not aware of any limit to how far we can travel through time or in space. I've apparently flown hundreds of light years away from Earth and experienced no deleterious effect upon my consciousness or to my physical body. It seems that as far as an OBE is concerned, down the street is no different than down the galaxy. I've found that OBE speed of flight is tempered by the scale of distance we want to travel. This may correlate with the speed of our ability to process information. When flying through a nonphysical city I could fly only as fast as a speeding vehicle. Flying through outer space I reached speeds of *trillions* of miles per second. It's like how when traveling in our automobile there is a rough maximum speed at which we feel *comfortable* traveling, though it may not be the maximum speed of the automobile we are traveling with. During the out-of-body experience there seems to be a self-imposed comfort scale to speed, according to the environment we are flying through. So I imagine that if I had a goal to visit a galaxy hundreds of *galaxies* away I could fly by galaxies in the same way that I have flown by stars.

In an attempt to calculate the fastest I have ever flown I recalled the experience of apparently going to planet Thiaoouba, after visiting The Source. And any current math and/or science whizzes out there, feel free to write me and correct any errors in these calculations. About 5 stars were going by per second. I have found online that there are about 4 to 5 light years between stars *on average* in the Milky Way galaxy.[37] [38] So if we say 4.5 light years between stars, and I was traveling by about five stars per second, that means I was traveling about *22.5 light years per second.* Over the course of a year light travels about 5,878,499,810,000 miles (5 trillion, 878 billion, 499 million, 810 thousand miles).[39] So over the course of 22 ½ years light travels 132,266,245,725,000 miles (132 trillion, 266 billion, 245 million, 725 thousand miles) – that means I was traveling at speeds of *over 132 trillion miles per second.* I suppose I traveled for about 10 seconds, so that would mean I traveled about 225 light years, or over 1.3 quadrillion miles.[40]

There's about 93,000,000 miles between Earth and our Sun,[41] which means I traveled about the equivalent of going back and forth between Earth and our Sun over 14 million times, over the course of about 10 seconds. At far as linear flight goes as stated I'm sure this is nowhere near top speed – and of course teleportation is instantaneous.

The Milky Way galaxy is about 110,000 light years across on average.[42] That would mean I traveled about 1/500

---

[37] https://www.google.com/search?q=distance+between+stars; http://www.itwire.com/science-news/space/57280-astronomers-find-average-distance-between-stars

[38] Light speed is the speed of a beam of light through a vacuum, about 186,000 miles per second. A *light year* is the distance a beam of light travels through a vacuum over the course of a year.

[39]   http://www.universetoday.com/65644/how-far-is-a-lightyear-in-miles/

[40] 1, 322, 662, 457, 250, 000.

[41]   http://www.space.com/17081-how-far-is-earth-from-the-sun.html

[42] en.wikipedia.org/wiki/Milky_Way

the diameter of the galaxy – which would make that planet pretty close. I wonder if my estimations could be off – for instance on how many stars I passed by per second, or how long I was traveling. It's possible that I went to a planet similar to the *state of being* I was seeking; an advanced planet. Both Darryl Anka and Lyssa Royal speak of an advanced race of extraterrestrials residing in the Pleiades constellation, which is only about 444 light years away from Earth.[43] It's possible I saw a planet in that system.

THE NONPHYSICAL WORLD

There's a subjective nature to the out-of-body experience, especially in the higher dimensional nonphysical worlds. We perceive energy, and then translate that energy into forms we understand. That's why at one time in society nonphysical explorers talked about the "River Styx" that took people to the underworld, whereas today people might speak of a train or bus taking them to different areas of the afterlife. And we also will allow into our understanding only what we will accept. This even happens in daily physical life, which we take to be static and immutable. This is important to keep in mind so that we don't allow false interpretations to sully our perceptions and experiences. It's very possible to misinterpret things perceived, or to cloud perceptions with our own projections. Open-mindedness and cross-validation is important.

The out-of-body experience is a tool; a great tool, but like any tool its use depends on the user. Usually the *essence* of any observation remains, for instance whether it's a ferryman taking someone by boat to the underworld, or a bus or train operator ferrying someone over land, the *essence* of

---

[43] http://en.wikipedia.org/wiki/Pleiades

being carried along a well-trodden path through the nonphysical to a stable nonphysical destination remains.

Always acknowledge every perception as you don't want to overlook something offhand because it doesn't fit your preconceptions. Even in remote viewing they note what is or could be their own projections – they just note it as such. When in doubt look to the *essence* of the perception for interpretation. And if unsure see if you can corroborate the perception or experience with other travelers. Collate all the data and cross-validate when you can.

REAL-TIME ENVIRONMENT

The real-time environment or the here-now is the experience of traveling through the physical world in the out-of-body state. Note my very first experience when I walked through walls and was able to perceive and confirm the actions of my mother in the kitchen. One notable variable during real-time travel may be variations in color compared to our in-body observations of the physical world. Notice that my childhood OBE walking experiences were in a monotone bluish-white color. Kurt Leland's early experiences were often in a monotone sepia color, like a Daguerreotype photograph. It's as if my perceptions were like a bluish Daguerreotype whereas his were in sepia. Chris Burrows' visual perceptions were a kind of sepia, like old Daguerreotype photographs, as well. So a monochrome color scheme for the experience seems to be a regular thing. But this is usually when perceiving the outside world at night. Color seems more readily visible when perceiving an environment illuminated by sunlight.

Another very entertaining aspect of the real-time environment is the ability to visit places you may otherwise be *unable* to visit. These can be distant locations, such as monumental landmarks. It can be outer space locales, or deep under the sea. This can be combined with time travel to visit local or distant locations at different places on the timeline.

I've mentioned the common tendency to slip into nonphysical worlds when passing through walls or doors – you start walking through a door in your home and end up in a nonphysical realm. I'm not sure why sometimes I can walk through walls and end up on the other side of the wall just fine and other times I end up in a nonphysical realm. It seems to go in waves, where sometimes I'm sort of stuck in the here-now world and other times I'm sort of stuck in nonphysical realms. One way you can circumvent ending up in nonphysical realms when going through physical barriers is to teleport to where you want to go.

NONPHYSICAL REALMS

My experience of the higher dimensional worlds is that they are made like a honeycomb. If one were to enter a nonphysical dimension it may look like a normal physical locale. But instead of a gradual and perceptible change of environment as one has traveling across a physical country, one instead experiences an abrupt change of environment. I had one experience where I became aware in a higher dimensional environment in a hotel, and ended up having sex with a nonphysical entity. I exited the building and explored, and decided to fly up to see what was above the nonphysical sky. What is found was that at a certain point the blue sky turned into the depths of a body of water. When I flew up to the surface of the water I hit a solid surface like ice, which I broke through into a nonphysical area that resembled a cold climate Earth location. In another experience I became aware in a nonphysical area that resembled an average farm in the physical world. I flew continuously in one direction and experienced a sudden change to a city-like environment. I continued to fly in the same direction and flew through several different areas, experiencing the abrupt change in environment. I began to explore the actual point of change or shift. I found a wall of grayish inert energy, a sort of *barrier zone*, on either side of which were two distinct regions of the nonphysical. Some of these barrier zones are paper thin, while some are several feet thick.

My observation is that this inert non-nonphysical matter is the same energy that constitutes the nonphysical dimensions themselves. In applying the Place-There Visualization technique I have several times established quite stable nonphysical environments and found that when I failed to maintain them by visiting or visualizing them regularly they began to deteriorate into the same inert nonphysical energy. I imagine that the areas that are maintained by the minds and intentions of several entities deteriorate in the same way if all said entities were to cease inhabiting and reinforcing that region.

THE VOID

A common experience in meditation or trance is of being in a field or expanse of apparent nothingness. It can be likened to outer space without stars, or a vast emptiness that almost has substance. This experience can extend from a mere visual experience to the experience of actually hovering in or floating in the void. When actually floating or being in the void you are effectively in the OBE state, and can intend yourself to a specific location in the physical world or the nonphysical dimension.

THE M-BAND

Robert Monroe spoke of M-Band noise, an area of the nonphysical made up of the random and disorganized thoughts of the inhabitants of Earth. Given that humanity as a whole is in such discord, as well as is very mentally undertrained, it is not surprising that the combined thoughts of humanity make a great cacophony of noise. I've experienced this noise several times as I've gone through the stages toward OBE. Somewhere in the theta state range I would become aware of a large amount of chatter, as if I were in a party and listening to all the different conversations going on in the room. The chatter sounded as if it was somehow 2 or 3 feet above floor level, as if slightly elevated relative to the physical world.

THE PARK

A place famously introduced by Robert Monroe is The Park, a nonphysical area where people who are not heavily invested in any religious belief about the afterlife might go after death. It's near the location of the large nonphysical university where sleeping people may unconsciously go to learn and socialize, as well as near the Akashic Records building.

THE AKASHIC RECORDS

The Akashic Records is described as an area of the nonphysical where all information about everything in existence can be accessed. As stated before about interpretation, apparently it takes a form that is understandable to the thinking of the one accessing it, often in our time appearing as a library filled with shelves of books. Outside it looks like a large mansion with columns in front. Inside there is an atrium area with a glass ceiling and balcony, and shelves of books that all appear to be hardcover in a brown, very nondescript cover. I don't think it's necessary to go here via OBE to access all information, as there is really only one mind in existence and every seemingly separate person, place, and thing is a part of it. I think just like the silver cord idea, we fashion forms to symbolize certain functions and abilities in ways that we can understand. The Essassani extraterrestrial race seem to access the Akashic Records all the time, as they have the ability to simply *know* what they need to know whenever they need to know it.

THE UNIVERSITY

The University is a location of nonphysical learning that people go to, apparently consciously *and* unconsciously. One of the people I saw there, a fellow high school student at the time, seemed quite conscious while there. Yet the next day at school it seemed as if she had no awareness of seeing me there, which means she probably doesn't remember being there at all. Robert Monroe spoke of "sleeper's classes" that people unconsciously, nonphysically attend while their bodies are in deep sleep. Apparently when you start to consciously visit the nonphysical worlds such classes are no longer necessary – or by then what they teach has already been learned. One time Monroe happened upon a sleeper's class and was told he needn't be there anymore.

TIME AND SPACE DURING OBE

You have probably heard that there is no such thing as time and space in the nonphysical dimensions and during the out-of-body state. I find that this is not true – unless it also means to say that there is no time and space in the physical world either. There is an ability to travel *through* time, unbounded by time, with the OBE, yet the experience of quantifiable sequence is still there. And a field within which distinct objects can be discerned is still there. Otherwise each time we got out of body we'd see ourselves getting out all of the other times we got out. If there was no space in the experience we'd be everywhere at once when we entered the OBE, or there'd be nowhere to go. It is easy to confuse the ability to circumvent linearity and space with the working nonexistence of time or space.

Our physical world experiences are not as temporally and spatially static as we often believe them to be. We regularly speed up time, slow down time, and skip over space in our experience even in the physical world, according to how we use our consciousness. We've all experienced the common saying that "time flies when you're having fun." It is actually quite true that when we are very focused or very involved in what we're doing we actually change the flow of our movement through time. We've all experienced getting places sooner than we "should" have – we can actually skip over space. In truth the physical world and the nonphysical world are simply different forms of the same dream, and the "laws" of physics can be both circumvented or obeyed in either, being that those laws are wholly illusory. By agreement we usually interact with the ideas of time and space in certain ways, to make a certain type of experience.

Through OBE I've gone both into the past and into the future – including into an alternate timeline. My friend Louis regularly travels into the future to see what will happen to him, for instance who he will meet before he meets them physically. It's also possible to explore alternate timelines to see what happens in other versions of Earth. The way I've accomplished time travel and alternate timeline travel is through teleportation, by simply intending *when* I wanted to go, or what difference in history I wanted to explore. Time travel can also happen spontaneously so that you don't know when you are during the experience, but may be able to put together the clues to find out later.

16 – OTHERWORLDLY INHABITANTS

There are a host of nonphysical inhabitants you will encounter during your travels. Some of these are actually physical beings whose physical reality corresponds to our nonphysical vibration – sometimes naturally according to dimensional differences, and sometimes due to advanced technology. Here is an example of some of the types of beings you might experience.

SPIRIT GUIDES

Apparently there are entities in the nonphysical that solely guide and teach both individuals who are still incarnate in the physical world and those who are deceased and solely in the nonphysical. People describe these as sometimes being deceased relatives from the same lifetime they are living. Other times they may be acquaintances from other lifetimes, from different Earth cultures, or even an extraterrestrial culture. Often times our guides will be different versions of ourselves – for instance a future version of our current self, or from a different sometimes extraterrestrial lifetime. Lyssa Royal's and Darryl Anka's guides are both ETs that are future incarnations of themselves, and who they have to some degree seen in person. Darryl saw their craft in broad daylight (with other witnesses) and Lyssa even had in-person contact. And sometimes conversely *we* may meet other versions of ourselves in order to guide and help them. Robert Monroe went into the past via the out-of-body experience to help himself; at the time his younger self didn't realize it was him. Gary Renard experiences visits from in a sense future versions of himself – ascended masters in the form of his next lifetime and that of his mate in that lifetime. The notion of seeing trans-temporal versions of ourselves is quite profound and apparently quite frequent.

OTHER TRAVELERS

A very practical and interesting experience is to meet other conscious out-of-body explorers. Most of your encounters with others might find them unconscious or with no memory of the experience. I'm sure this is changing though. But if you can arrange to meet up with a conscious out-of-body explorer you can exchange information and then confirm the interaction afterwards. I remember reading of a couple on Alfred Ballabene's website; they would meet nightly and continue the day's conversation during the out-of-body state, and then continue the out-of-body conversation when back in-body the next day. Another frequent partnered explorer is Bruce Moen, who frequently travelled with a companion who showed him around the afterlife, and who regularly validated the experience through the sharing of her side of their nonphysical interactions. Time and again their experiences matched perfectly, just as it would if you physically went to a location with someone and later share and corroborate what you saw and did there.

NONPHYSICAL LOCALS

This category of nonphysical inhabitant can take a variety of forms. It could be a newly deceased relative or friend, or all different manner of life that you might not even recognize as sentient. Recall the 'tube entity' I encountered in one of my journeys, as well as the 'box-being' I encountered in another. And this is not to mention the host of extraterrestrial beings that are to be encountered there. Some look nearly human, and some are clearly not human. Some ET's apparently exists physically in our nonphysical, whereas some are simply out-of-body like we are.

Some extraterrestrial contact experiences that we may *think* are dreams or out-of-body experiences are actually physical interactions that we perceive through a very dreamy altered state. High level ETs operate in the alpha to theta range of consciousness, and act as magnets that draw us into a relative state. They step down their vibrations some, and we're naturally drawn up in vibration some, and we meet somewhere in between. Our degree of functionality and awareness depends upon how trained we are to develop a flexibility of consciousness. The regular practice of state acquisition would allow more clarity and wakefulness in these physical encounters.

One of the most intriguing altered state experiences I've had was after watching the movie *A.I.* produced by Steven Spielberg. The movie was so profound, and had such an emotional impact upon me, that after witnessing the brilliant and heart-wrenching ending I was in an enormously high emotional state. I'd decided right then that I wanted to meet someone or something of a higher or more advanced spiritual nature, face to face right then. I had a deep and intense longing for some type of higher connection. I was so intent in this that I'd decided that I would sit there, and focus and intend on receiving the audience of some higher level being, and that *I would not move*, and would not let go of focusing my intention until I did, even if it meant dying of thirst and starvation; I would not budge until someone or something showed. I focused harder, and with more determination by the minute, and grew more and more resolute. And then suddenly, and surprisingly, a being walked into my bedroom *through* the wall. I was so shocked and taken aback that I didn't even open my physical eyes. I was squeezing them shut as I focused to see instead with my inner eye – the inner perceptions seemed more vital or valid at the time; or perhaps I was afraid of what I might see. Whoever or whatever this being was, it's very presence was palpable and tangible, as if it was made of radiant and palpable electromagnetism.

I paused my mental calling and made my mind alert to it, not sure what to do next. I imagine that the being noticed my shocked and somewhat frightened state, and simply withdrew back through the wall from whence it emerged. I sat there amazed that a being really did show up. Beings really are around, and they listen and hear us. And if sincere in asking, they will even show up to greet you. *Be prepared*.

17 – OBE AND METAPHYSICS

SPIRITUALITY AND ENLIGHTENMENT

When I began to understand what I was experiencing I thought that the out-of-body experience held the key to spiritual evolution. I was wrong. The out-of-body experience is *not* in and of itself a spiritual experience. It is a method or mode of perception and experience – *a very useful* mode of perception where we allow ourselves to perceive and experience outside and beyond the usual self-imposed constraints of space and time, but a mode of perception and experience nonetheless. It can be *applied* to spiritual ends; but this is the same with any other device or skill or experience or ability. But the ability to out-of-body travel in and of itself is *not* spiritual. Nothing perceivable or conceivable or part of the world of time, space, form, and perception can be spiritual. The spiritual is *totally beyond* time, space, perception, and form of any kind – including nonphysical or energetic form, however nebulous or fluid those forms may be.

One of the ways OBE can be utilized to help further spiritual development is to help expand our understanding of ourselves and the universe, and thus help us to *reinterpret* the world and our lives in more expanded ways. *The true key to spiritual advancement is in the ways we interpret our lives.* Do you interpret the world from a place of separation, attack, fear, anger, hate, and prejudice, or do you interpret the world from a place of oneness, sameness, peace, love, forgiveness, gentleness, and acceptance? A recognition that we are consciousness, a state of being shared with *everyone* regardless of form – even other-dimensional and extraterrestrial beings, can have a profound effect upon how we interpret the world. And we can recognize this and still live normal and engaged physical lives. We can still defend ourselves and others, and eat the foods we like, and have interactions and relations with others. But rather than hating people for differences of physical form, or culture, or whatever, we can embrace those differences, being aware of our oneness beyond *all* physical world characteristics.

ASCENSION AND HEALING

I eventually learned of an idea called *ascension* whereby one elevates their vibrations to the point of being able to "ascend" or take oneself physically through to higher dimensions (an idea different from the idea of an "ascended master," which is the reappearance of an enlightened being who has died, such as the beings who appear to Gary Renard). Supposedly J Z Knight channels an ancient being who accomplished dimensional ascension through extensive out-of-body traveling. I haven't experienced this yet, but I do believe that it's possible. It has been technologically done by ETs with their interstellar craft, and technology normally mimics the mind.[44] I do have some interesting experiences to let me know that we can and do have a profound effect upon the physical world through nonphysical means, including through use of altered states and the out-of-body experience.

I remember an experience where I meditated on the roof of a building. I sat in the Indian Pose asana and stimulated the chakras of my hands, and then drew energy up my arms and into my crown chakra. I stimulated my crown chakra. I then drew energy up my arms and through my crown and down into my brow chakra. I then stimulating my brow chakra. I repeated this process down my front centerline of chakras. At one point I suddenly realized the wind was no

---

[44] *The Disappearance of the Universe,* page 7

longer blowing. I stopped my practice to pay attention to my physical environment and suddenly the wind hit me all at once. To test the experience I went back into an altered state and again it was total silence, with no feeling or sound of the wind. Immediately upon coming out of the altered state I was again abruptly hit by a wall of air. My experience was that the meditation was so deep and the energy field built so strong that my aura prevented the wind from hitting my physical body. When I came out of the meditation the field collapsed and the air hit me again. It could also have been that in my altered state I simply could not *perceive* the feel and sound of the wind against me. But my experience at the time was that a field of inactivity surrounding me collapsed when I came out of meditation, allowing the wind to reach my physical body.

I've also utilized altered states to help enact great physical healing. Decades ago I used to have hepatitis B. I used deep meditative states to help clear my body of the disease; among other things such as drinking lots of water and energy working. I would sit and reach an altered state by relaxing and feeling for the energy of my body. I would reach such a state that the energy flow would build so that I would perceive the actual meridians and channels along which the energy travels through my body. It was as if my physical body disappeared and I was aware *only* of a grid of energy strengthening and reinforcing a healthy template upon which my physical body would reorient itself. After about two years of the practice at one point I knew my body was clear. I could *feel* it. I went and took various in-depth medical tests and it was found that I am clear of hepatitis B and that I have developed immunity. I've verified my health several times since my initial test. During another period of metaphysical experimentation I practiced telekinesis on clouds. Using intent and visualization I could cause a circle of cloudless sky to expand and open in the overcast sky.

In my research I found a lady named Niro Asistent, who through meditation, diet change, and various other life and thought changes, healed herself of HIV, verified several times through medical examination. I've also come across accounts of people with so-called multiple personality disorder exhibiting drastic physiological changes between personalities. For instance one personality would have cancer and another would not, one personality would have certain color eyes and another would have different color eyes, one personality would be sickly and frail and another healthy and extremely strong. These *physical traits* would change as the person switched between personalities! Even the chemical and hormonal composition of the body varied between personalities. It is apparent that the extent of our influence upon the physical world, including our own bodies, is as broad as we allow it to be.

OTHER LIFETIMES

So much of our errors in perceiving ourselves and others could be alleviated if only it were common knowledge on Earth that we experience several lifetimes. How could someone justify hating another person because of the color of their skin when they are aware they have personally experienced several lifetimes as a person with that same type of skin? How could a person hate another culture being aware that they have experienced living several lifetimes as a member of that very culture? Gender, culture, skin color, religious belief, location, class, wealth or lack thereof – I am certain that almost all of us have experienced several lifetimes as each. Very few beings experience only one or two lifetimes on Earth. Most of us experience *thousands*. The idea of reincarnation was even in the Christian Bible at one time, but was removed by church leaders for their own purposes.[45] This delay in global paradigm shift to recognize the idea of multiple lifetimes could be because we are all so invested in keeping the illusion of differences and separation intact, so that we have someone or something seemingly separate or different to especially love or especially hate.

Brian Weiss is a psychotherapist who for years regressed patients into the memory of other lifetimes. He happened upon it when, regressing a patient back to the source of current psychological discord, the patient began to describe occurrences quite foreign to the current lifetime. Many of his patients were able to validate their memories, by finding locations and objects remembered through their regressions, some even finding descendants of their other incarnations who validated their memories. The psychological and physiological self we usually identify with is *not* who or what we are. As stated previously, the very idea of an individual self or ego is actually a false construct, maintained by denial and repression so that we can experience ourselves as finite beings. Learning to interpret the world from the level of shared identity is part and parcel of true spirituality.

If everyone on Earth were able to astral travel at will I'm certain that many of the ills that mar our society, and have marred Earth society for generations, would be shown as outmoded nonsense. The shift to recognizing *every* human being as a fragment of universal consciousness temporarily inhabiting a physical body would be great progress. We're moving in this direction, and beyond. The more of us who develop OBE ability and apply it to expanding our awareness and self-identity, being that *we all* make the world (however much we may want to blame the world's problems on small

---

[45] *The Disappearance of the Universe,* 319

groups of people), the more Earth paradigm shifts into a direction of peace and universal brotherhood.

ETS, IDS, AND CONTACT

When something enters our awareness or experience that is foreign to the vibrational signature of Earth, like an extraterrestrial craft or an extraterrestrial being, if our consciousness is not flexible or fluid enough to accommodate the experience it can be very disconcerting. We can lose awareness, fall asleep, become dizzy, become frightened, withdraw into ourselves, cover the experience with a false memory, or simply compartmentalize psychologically and have no memory of the experience. When I saw that craft near my home it was *so clear* that it was foreign – not of this dimension, or planet, or both. I didn't have such dramatic reactions during my childhood experiences. Perhaps I didn't really notice the vibrational differences because I thought that such experiences were very common, and perhaps that's why I was open and psychologically flexible to the experience. Or perhaps through frequently having such experiences at the time I was assimilated to foreign or extraterrestrial energy. It could also be that at the time I hadn't fully embraced *this* lifetime. All of our limits are ultimately self-imposed. And those early experiences were apparently very brief, so I imagine there's very much I don't recall from that childhood string of experiences.

State acquisition develops the *flexibility of consciousness* necessary to remain conscious enough in the altered states of alpha, theta, and delta – the states extraterrestrial and interdimensional contact causes dips into. But the necessary flexibility to fully experience and remember the encounter *also* includes the recognition of a unifying factor beyond all apparent differences: the unifying fundamental factor of consciousness or mind as discussed in previous sections. The more we experience and interpret life with this fundamental unifying principle in mind, the less "foreign" will foreign energy seem, and the less substantial will apparent differences be interpreted and experienced. Thus extraterrestrial and interdimensional life will seem less "different," and less "foreign," and more easily embraced and incorporated into our everyday lives. Thus the ultimate practicing ground for extraterrestrial/interdimensional contact is right here on Earth, in how we think about and relate to each other.

Steven Greer, after reaching a meditative state of cosmic consciousness, had an extended interaction with extraterrestrial beings. The craft he saw was of the same type of craft he saw at 9 years old. *Even with* his recently experienced state of cosmic awareness he initially withdrew into a childlike and fearful mental state. He ended up on their craft in outer space, and overcame the trepidation, and they meditated together – Greer and a small group of the ETs. He goes on to say:

"They [the ETs he meditated with] know that the only chance for peace on Earth -- never mind the cosmos -- is for humans to understand there's no real difference amongst us... What really matters is that within us lives the same singular light of consciousness... whether we're open to it or not at any given moment in time. It is the basis of our relationship with each other and with the universe... that is what we [in our meditation] experienced in its absolute, purest form... They didn't care about such things as age, race, family of origin, or wealth... There is really one people in the universe, and we are they. There is a single conscious being shining in all of us. It can never be divided, no matter how much we try... In a real sense, then, the heart of compassion and the foundation of peace is found in the reality that we are all one... the world's problems are essentially spiritual, therefore the solutions must be spiritual as well. And so it has turned out to be."[46]

If you would like to learn more about extraterrestrials, interdimensionals, and interactions with them, I'm working on a book entitled *Exo-Communications* to contain my further research, investigations, methods, and encounters. If you are or can be in the northern Kentucky area of the United States, or would like to sponsor me to come to your area of the world, you could come along with me as I initiate further ET/ID contacts, and further experiment and refine the practice. I intend to forge conscious interplanetary and interdimensional relationships as an ambassador to the stars, and to solidify contact protocols for *Exo-Communications*. Information is available through www.nextdensity.com. And perhaps you have some experiences you'd like to share. Contact me through my website at www.darryleberryjr.com.

I suggest studying the Bashar material channeled by Darryl Anka – including his book *Bashar* or *Quest for Truth*,[47] the Sasha, Germane, and Traveler material channeled by Lyssa Royal – including her book *Preparing for Contact*;[48] and the Sirius Disclosure movie facilitated by Dr. Steven Greer of the Disclosure Project and Sirius Disclosure, as well as his many interviews and speeches online – including his book *Hidden Truth: Forbidden Knowledge*.[49]

When the dominant reality frequency for Earth humanity becomes alpha and theta everyone will be able to jump through the various realities at will.[50] *The time is now to initiate this species-wide shift with our own individual*

---

[46] *Hidden Truth: Forbidden Knowledge* by Dr. Steven Greer, excerpts from Chapter 2.

[47] www.bashar.org

[48] www.lyssaroyal.net/

[49] www.siriusdisclosure.com

[50] *Preparing for Contact*, Lyssa Royal

practices and explorations and broadened universal interpretations. We may even open up perception and awareness of new realities and dimensions, and new corresponding brain wave states and psychological and physiological conditions.

APPENDIX

OBE/AP RESEARCH STUDY

In June through July of 2012 I initiated a two-month practical research study into the out-of-body experience, to further validate and refine the techniques shared in this work. I called it the **DEBJ's "Beyond the Body" Practical OBE Research Study**. This first phase, *Phase Alpha*, focused on validating and refining these methods in preparation for teaching a larger audience. I taught the *Travel Far* methodologies and techniques to 21 different participants. (Along the way several ceased participating for various reasons.) They let me know the number of basics practices and OBE sessions done per day through a checklist I provided. Participants were instructed to keep a brief but detailed journal of practices, which would help memory and recall, and to provide me this data so I could see what's going on in their progress, and so I could advise them and update any procedures as necessary. Everyone who participated as instructed at the least experienced altered state phenomenon, including sounds, voices, visual imagery, lucid dreams, and/or energetic sensations – showing that with continued practice success will be achieved. Several participants experienced indications of being on the verge of an out-of-body experience by the end of the Study. Overall 5 OBEs were reported by participants – 4 partial OBEs (a limb jutting free for instance), and 1 brief but full OBE that included the perception of a nonphysical entity. If you would like this sort of instruction and coaching I'll be continuing *and enhancing* this format as a 2-month intensive group course. Information is available through www.nextdensity.com.

LIST OF ILLUSTRATIONS

GLOSSARY OF TERMS

afterlife, the – the area of the nonphysical dimension that minds or souls or consciousness usually inhabit after the physical body has died and before the next lifetime.

akashic records – an area of the nonphysical dimension symbolic of our ability to access all information. In today's society it usually takes the form of a grand library.

altered state – a state characterized by the relaxation or sleep of the physical body and an alertness or wakefulness of the mind or consciousness.

altered state phenomena – any of various perceptions and experiences had during altered states, such as energetic vibrations, roaring sounds, visual imagery, floating sensations, etcetera.

asana – a meditative body position.

ascension – the ability to take one's physical body through to other dimensions; the state of having achieved such skill.

astral body – see nonphysical body.

astral projection; astral travel – see out-of-body experience.

barrier zone – an opaque but permeable barrier of inert nonphysical matter dividing two distinct areas of the nonphysical dimension.

brain wave state – the brain's functions observed as oscillations of electrical activity, called brain waves. The frequency of oscillation corresponds to different *states of consciousness* – generally beta (waking), alpha (relaxing), theta (meditation or light sleep), and delta (deep sleep or coma).

chakra – a focus and transfer point of energy in the nonphysical body; the nonphysical equivalent of bodily organs.

channeling – the process of accessing higher or inner sources of information or inspiration through nonphysical means such as telepathy or intuition.

consciousness – the basis of individual identity and awareness; experienced individually as the conscious energy at the core of sentient life forms.

dimension – a broad range of frequency of matter and energy, making a discernable strata or realm in the continuum of space-time. One example of a dimension is the physical dimension, characterized by certain limitations such as movement bound by gravity, speed limited to the speed of light, etcetera; as opposed to the nonphysical dimension characterized by less limitation. Interstellar extraterrestrial spacecraft often switch to a nonphysical dimension, traverse or circumvent space free of the speed limits of the physical dimension, and then drop back down into the physical dimension at their destination.

energy work (e-work) – the practice of stimulating and manipulating the energy body.

etheric body – see nonphysical body.

extraterrestrial – of or from beyond the biosphere or orbit of Earth. This can be a meteor or a race of beings from another solar system. Often abbreviated as ET.

fail-safe – a mechanism whereby if extremely afraid or overwhelmed during an out-of-body experience one is suddenly sucked back into or catapulted back to the physical body.

flexibility of consciousness – the characteristic of being able to access a wide range of states of consciousness while remaining consciously aware and retaining memory of the experience.

focus level – a delineation system made by Robert Monroe to differentiate between different levels of altered states, and different dimensional levels of experience. The basic altered state is focus 10 or F10, the state of deep trance or mind awake/body asleep; 12 is a state of expanded awareness; 15, an experience of no time; 21, the edge of the physical dimension where one accesses nonphysical or other-dimensional systems; 22, where humans in comas or delirium situate themselves; 23, where the recently deceased congregate; 24-26, where people congregate who believe in certain religions – the nonphysical areas are constructed by and according to their afterlife beliefs; 27, the level of the Park, the University, and the Akashic Records building; 28 is beyond or outside the human range – to permanently reside beyond this point one gives up being human. Each of these levels can be experienced through application of the *Travel Far* methodologies.

hypnagogic / hypnopompic imagery – hypnagogic is a word to describe the state of consciousness as one goes into sleep, and hypnopompic is a word to describe the state of consciousness as one comes out of sleep. As one passes through the theta state the visual imagery perceived is called either hypnagogic or hypnopompic depending upon whether one is going into sleep or waking from sleep.

ident – a memory built up to serve as a locator of a target one would like to OBE to. For instance, if a person, what the person looks like, how they smell, their attitude, their likes and dislikes, etcetera.

in-between lifetime realms – see afterlife, the.

interdimensional – of or from beyond the dimensional range normally experienced by the third density / fourth dimensional Earth. This can be from nonphysical dimensions as well as parallel universes. I often abbreviate this as ID.

invisible helper – a nonphysical explorer who helps others while OBE.

light being – an entity perceived to be made of light. Sometimes the being is actually made of light, and other times differences in vibration can make a being *seem* to be made of light.

lucid dreaming – the experience of being consciously aware during a nocturnal dream.

M-band noise – the area of the nonphysical comprised of the thought radiation of humanity, which due to the disordered state of the average human psyche is like a cacophony of noise.

mantra – a word, phrase, or syllable(s) mentally repeated as a meditation or focusing fixative.

missing time – a period of apparently no memory in relation to an extraterrestrial or interdimensional encounter.

mudra – a meditative hand position.

nonphysical – the levels of existence that are finer and higher vibratory than the physical world.

nonphysical body – the ephemeral energy-based body we can experience ourselves in during out-of-body experiences. It is often called the astral body or the etheric body. Some distinguish the energy body we experience with energy work as the etheric body, and the energy body we OBE with as the astral body.

out-of-body experience – the experience of existing and perceiving apart from the physical body, usually as an energy-based body similar in appearance to the physical body or as a point or field of consciousness. Commonly abbreviated as OBE, or OOBE.

parallel processing – accessing two or more states of consciousness simultaneously, for instance being consciously engaged in the out-of-body experience while also perceiving through or orchestrating with the physical body.

paralysis – the pre- and post-OBE state of being unable to move. It is a common and natural occurrence of deep sleep, apparently to stop the physical acting out of dreams during sleep.

physical – a dense level of existence which is the lowest and slowest of a continuum of vibration and frequency and matter.

pineal gland – a pinecone shaped gland in the center of the brain, supposedly to some degree responsible for various psychic abilities.

portal – an area in the nonphysical that acts as a teleportation mechanism or wormhole, either between different points in a dimension or between different dimensions.

repercussion – the experience of abrupt shaking of the physical body following a rapid nonphysical reentry into the physical body.

rote – packets of nonphysical information; the nonphysical equivalent to books. These information packets can be transmitted, received, and stored, and unraveled and learned at a later time.

screen – the mental space perceived during meditation; the visual field within or upon which visual imagery forms.

screen memory – a false memory used to cover over an encounter with extraterrestrial or interdimensional beings. The contactee or the beings can be responsible for such memories – I suspect that in various encounters and depending upon the beings encountered it could be either or both.

sleeper's classes / schools – classes in the nonphysical for incarnates during sleep. The classes are rarely if ever remembered, but the information learned still helps through the subconscious or unconscious mind.

space-time – the universal field within which all physical and nonphysical activity occurs. The more nonphysical the activity the less bound by limits of speed, motion, and location in time or space.

state acquisition – the practice of consciously entering the alpha, theta, and/or delta brain wave states, including all relaxation and meditation practices. This also includes gamma, but gamma is peripheral to developing out-of-body ability.

state of consciousness – the dimensional focus of conscious awareness. Generally there are two different focuses, the waking physical world focus of the beta brain wave state, and the altered state focus including alpha, theta, and delta states.

telepathy / telempathy – the transference of ideas and thoughts through nonphysical means. Bashar sometimes calls it "telempathy" saying the emotions are heavily involved in the process.

trance – see altered state.

transdimensional – see interdimensional.

vibrations – the experience of vibrating during sleep or altered states, caused by the increased flow of energy natural to conscious altered states.

visual imagery – see hypnagogic / hypnopompic imagery.

void, the – an area of the nonphysical characterized by a deep, featureless blackness, like outer space without stars.

BIBLIOGRAPHY

There are many books I've read or gained relevant morsels of information from through the years that I don't remember the title for, or remember the author of. Those that stood out in my memory, or were easier to find, are listed here.

A Course in Astral Travel and Dreams by Beelzebub (Aug 10, 2005)

Abduction to the 9th Planet by Michel Desmarquet

Adventures Beyond the Body: How to Experience Out-of-Body Travel by William Buhlman (May 24, 1996)

Adventures in Consciousness: An Introduction to Aspect Psychology (Classics in Consciousness Series Book) by Jane Roberts (Nov 1, 2005)

Art and Practice of Astral Projection, The by Ophiel (1967)

Art of Dreaming, The by Carlos Castaneda (May 19, 1994)

Astral Body: And Other Astral Phenomena, The by A.E. Powell (January 1, 1927)

Astral Dynamics: A New Approach to Out-Of-Body Experiences by Robert Bruce (Nov 1, 1999)

Astral Plane, The (Theosophical Manual No. 5) by C. W. Leadbeater and C. Jinarajadasa (1972)

Astral Plane, The by Arthur E. Powell (Dec 1, 2005)

Astral Plane: Its Scenery, Inhabitants and Phenomena, The by C. W. Leadbeater

Astral Projection and Psychic Empowerment: Techniques for Mastering the Out-Of-Body Experience by Joe H. Slate (Dec 8, 1998)

Astral Projection by Oliver Fox (Jun 1, 2000)

Astral Projection for Beginners: Six Techniques for Traveling to Other Realms by Edain McCoy (Mar 8, 1999)

Astral Projection Workbook: How to Achieve Out-Of-Body Experiences, The by James H. Brennan (Jun 30, 1990)

Astral Projection: A Record of Out of the Body Experiences by Oliver Fox (Jun 1993)

Astral Travel for Beginners: Transcend Time and Space with Out-of-Body Experiences by Richard Webster (Sep 8, 2002)

Astral Travel: Your Guide to the Secrets of Out-Of-The-Body Experiences by Yvonne Frost and Gavin Frost (Jun 1, 1985)

Astral Voyages: Mastering the Art of Soul Travel by Bruce Goldberg (Oct 1999)

Astral World and Its Helpers, The by Yogi Ramacharaka

Autobiography of a Yogi by Paramhansa Yogananda

Awaken Healing Energy Through The Tao by Mantak Chia (June 1, 1983)

Baguazhang: Theory and Applications by Yang Jwing-Ming and Liang Shou-Yu (Aug 29, 2008)

Bashar: Blueprint for Change: A Message from Our Future by Darryl Anka (Dec 1990)

Beyond My Wildest Dreams: Diary of a UFO Abductee by Kim Carlsberg and Darryl Anka [Illustrator] (July 1, 1995)

Beyond the Body: An Investigation of Out-of-the-Body Experiences by Susan J. Blackmore (Aug 30, 2005)

Beyond the Occult by Colin Wilson. (1988, 1989, 2008)

Buckland's Complete Book of Witchcraft by Raymond Buckland

Candle Magick Workbook: Why and How Candle Magick Works Paperback, The by Kala Pajeon and Ketz Pajeon (August 1, 2000)

Case Book of Astral Projection, 545-746 by Robert Crookall (Apr 1980)

Chakras, The by C W Leadbeater

Christmas Message, by Samael Aun Weor (1967)

Clairvoyance and Occult Powers by Swami Panchadasi

Coming of Tan, The by Riley Martin and O-Qua Tangin Wann (1995)

Concentration: A Guide to Mental Mastery by Mouni Sadhu (1980)

Concentration: An Approach to Meditation (Quest Books) by Ernest Wood (Oct 18, 2007)

Cosmic Explorers by Courtney Brown

Cosmic Journeys: My Out-of-Body Explorations With Robert A. Monroe by Rosalind A. McKnight and Laurie A. Monroe (Mar 1, 1999)

Cosmic Voyage by Courtney Brown

Crystal River Flowing: Adventures in Co-Creation by Marilynn Hughes (Mar 1993)

Disappearance of the Universe, The by Gary R. Renard

Do_OBE: How to Lucid Dream, Astral Project and Have Out-of-Body Experiences by Donald DeGracia (Jan 1, 2006)

Dream Yoga: Consciousness, Astral Projection, and the Transformation of the Dream State by Samael Aun Weor (Mar 1, 2010)

Dreams, "Evolution", and Value Fulfillment, Vol. 1: A Seth Book by Seth, Jane Roberts and Robert F. Butts (Jun 19, 1997)

Eckankar: The Key to Secret Worlds by Paul Twitchell (1988)

Encounters on the Astral: A Personal Record of Out of Body Experiences by Chris Burrows (2000)

Essence of Taiji Qigong: The Internal Foundation of Taijiquan, The by Yang Jwing-Ming (Paperback - Aug 21, 1998)

Etheric Double: The Health Aura of Man, The by A E Powell (January 1, 1997)

Experiencing Astral Travel: An 8 Week Course by V. M. Beelzebub (May 1, 2003)

Explorations Out of the Body: A Beginner's Roadmap to the Universe by Eddie Slasher (May 1997)

Exploring the World of Lucid Dreaming by Stephen LaBerge and Howard Rheingold (Nov 13, 1991)

Far Journeys by Robert A. Monroe (Dec 1, 1992)

Fell's Know It All Guide to ESP Power by Jane Roberts (Apr 15, 2000)

Finding of the Third Eye, The by Vera Stanley Alder (1968)

Fire in the Sky: The Walton Experience by Travis Walton. (Aug 1997)

Flying Without a Broom: Astral Projection and the Astral World by D. J. Conway (Sep 8, 2002)

Galactica: A Treatise on Death, Dying and the Afterlife - by Marilynn Hughes (Nov 11, 2004)

Handbook of Astral Projection by Richard A. Greene (Jan 1985)

Hands of Light: A Guide to Healing Through the Human Energy Field by Barbara Brennan and Jos. A. Smith (May 1, 1988)

Have an Out-of-Body Experience in 30 Days, Second Edition: The Free Flight Program (30-Day Higher Consciousness) by Keith Harary Ph.D. and Pamela Weintraub (Mar 15, 1999)

Hercolubus or Red Planet by V. M. Rabolu (Oct 1, 2002)

Hidden Truth: Forbidden Knowledge by Steven M Greer (April 28, 2006)

Holographic Universe, The by Michael Talbot

How I Learned Soul Travel: The True Experiences of a Student in Eckankar, the Ancient Science of Soul Travel by Terrill Wilson and Terrill Willson (Jul 1997)

How to Travel to Other Dimensions by DragonStar and S. Panchadasi (Apr 2002)

Incidents in My Life by D D Home

Initiation by Elisabeth Haich (Seed Center, March 1994)

Invisibility & Levitation: How-To Keys To Personal Performance by Commander X and Tim R. Swartz (Apr 16, 2011)

Invisible Helpers by C. W. Leadbeater (Jun 20, 2007)

Journeys Out of the Body by Robert A. Monroe (Dec 1, 1992)

Leaving the Body: A Complete Guide to Astral Projection by D. Scott Rogo (Jan 1, 1993)

Lessons Out of the Body: A Journal of Spiritual Growth and Out-of-Body Travel by Robert Peterson (Jan 1, 2002)

Life After Death by Damien Echols (2011)

Light Emerging: The Journey of Personal Healing by Barbara Ann Brennan (Nov 1, 1993)

Living with the Himalayan Masters by Swami Rama

Llewellyn Practical Guide to Astral Projection: The Out-of-Body Experience, The by Melita; Phillips, Osborne Denning (1995)

Love Has Forgotten No One by Gary R. Renard (Oct 2013)

Magical Use of Thought Forms by Dolores Ashcroft-Nowicki (December 8, 2001)

Many Lives Many Masters by Brian L Weiss

Masquerade of Angels by Dr Karen Turner

Mastering Astral Projection: 90-day Guide to Out-of-Body Experience by Robert Bruce and Brian Mercer (Nov 8, 2004)

Matrix V, by The Author

Meditation by Mouni Sadhu

Mental Body, The by Arthur E. Powell

Mind Trek: Exploring Consciousness, Time, and Space Through Remote Viewing by Joseph McMoneagle (*September 1, 1993*)

My Big TOE - The Complete Trilogy by Thomas Campbell (2007)

Mysteries of the Redemption: A Treatise on Out-of-Body Travel and Mysticism, The by Marilynn Hughes (Nov 11, 2004)

Nature of Personal Reality: Specific, Practical Techniques for Solving Everyday Problems and Enriching the Life You Know, The by Jane Roberts and Robert F. Butts (May 17, 1994)

New Energy Ways, V2, by Robert Bruce (1999)

Odysseys of Light by Marilynn Hughes (Aug 1991)

Otherwhere: A Field Guide to Nonphysical Reality for the Out-of-Body Traveler by Kurt Leland (Jan 1, 2002)

Out of the Body Experiences: A Fourth Analysis by Robert Crookall (1970)

Out-Of-Body Adventures: 30 Days to the Most Exciting Experience of Your Life by Rick Stack (Sep 1, 1988)

Out-of-Body Experiences: How to Have Them and What to Expect by Robert Peterson and Charles Tart (Apr 1, 1997)

Out-of-Body Exploring: A Beginner's Approach by Preston Dennett (Aug 31, 2004)

Oversoul Seven Trilogy: The Education of Oversoul Seven, The Further Education of Oversoul Seven, Oversoul Seven and the Museum of Time, The by Jane Roberts (Jun 12, 1995)

Path Notes of an American Ninja Master by Glenn Morris

Perfect Love: Find Intimacy on the Astral Plane by D. J. Conway (Apr 8, 1998

Perfect Matrimony, or Door to Enter into Initiation, The by Samael Aun Weor (1950, 1961)

Personal Power through Awareness by Sanaya Roman

Pleiadian Workbook: Awakening Your Divine Ka, The by Amorah Quan Yin (Dec 1, 1995)

Power of Internal Martial Arts: Combat Secrets of Ba Gua, Tai Chi, and Hsing-I, The by Bruce Frantzis (Jan 19, 1998)

Practical Astral Projection by Yram (Jun 1974)

Practical Guide to Psychic Powers: Awaken Your Sixth Sense (Practical Guide Series) by Osborne Phillips and Melita Denning (Nov 8, 2000)

Practical Guide to Psychic Self-Defense by Melita Phillips and Osborne Denning

Practice of Magic, The by Draja Michaharic

Pranic Healing by Choa Kok Sui (Jun 1990)

Preparing for Contact: A Metamorphosis of Consciousness by Lyssa Royal and Keith Priest (1994, 2011)

Projectiology: A Panorama of Experiences of the Consciousness Outside the Human Body by Waldo Vieira (May 2002)

Projection of the Astral Body, The by Sylvan J. Muldoon (Apr 20, 2011)

Projections of the Consciousness by Waldo Vieira (Dec 17, 2007)

Psychic Development for Beginners: An Easy Guide to Releasing and Developing Your Psychic Abilities by William W. Hewitt (1996)

Psychic Discoveries Behind the Iron Curtain by Ostrander, Sheila; Schroeder, Lynn (1970)

Psychic Energy: How to Change Desires into Realities (Reward Classics) by Joseph J. Weed (Mar 1989)

Psychic Self-Defense by Dion Fortune

Psychic Vampires by Joe Slate

Ramtha: The White Book by Ramtha [J Z Knight]

Remote Perceptions: Out-of-Body Experiences, Remote Viewing, and Other Normal Abilities by Angela Thompson Smith (Nov 1, 1998)

Remote Viewing Secrets by Joseph McMoneagle (May 1, 2000)

Secret of the Soul: Using Out-of-Body Experiences to Understand Our True Nature by William Buhlman (Jul 3, 2001)

Seth Dreams and Projections of Consciousness by Jane Roberts (Aug 1998)

Sixth Sense: Including the Secrets of the Etheric Subtle Body by Stuart Wilde (Mar 1, 2000)

Soul Traveler: A Guide to Out-of-Body Experiences and the Wonders Beyond by Albert Taylor (Apr 1, 2000)

Study and Practice of Astral Projection, The by Robert Crookall (1973)

Successful Astral Projection To The Space And Universe by S. Sapphire (Dec 4, 2005)

Taijiquan, Classical Yang Style: The Complete Form and Qigong by Yang Jwing-Ming (Paperback - Apr 14, 1999)

Tale of the Body Thief, The by Anne Rice (Nov 17, 2010)

Talisman Magick Workbook: Master Your Destiny Through the Use of Talismans, The by Kala Pajeon (June 1, 2000)

Tao & The Tree of Life: Alchemical & Sexual Mysteries of the East & West, The by Eric Yudelove (Sep 8, 2002)

Teachings of Don Juan: A Yaqui Way of Knowledge, The Original Teachings, The by Carlos Castaneda (Sep 8, 1998)

The Kybalion: Hermetic Philosophy by Three Initiates (1940)

The Master Mind by Theron Q. Dumont

Thiaoouba Prophecy, The by Michel Desmarquet

Third Eye, The by T. Lobsang Rampa (Jun 12, 1986)

Thought Forms by C W Leadbeater

Thought Power by Annie Besant

Training to See Auras V4, by Robert Bruce (1990)

Trance Formation of America. Cathy O'Brien and Mark Phillips. (1995)

Traveling the Interstate of Consciousness: A Driver's Instruction Manual: Using Hemi-Sync to Access States of Non-Ordinary Reality by Patricia Leva (Jan 1, 1998)

Truth About Astral Projection, The by Keith Randolph (Sep 8, 2002)

Ultimate Journey, by Robert Monroe

Ultimate Time Machine, The by Joseph McMoneagle

Voyage Beyond Doubt by Bruce Moen (Nov 1, 1998)

Voyage to Curiosity's Father by Bruce Moen

Voyages into the Afterlife by Bruce Moen (Oct 1, 1999)

Voyages into the Unknown by Bruce Moen

Why I Survive AIDS by Niro Markoff Asistent (1991)

Wisdom of the Mystic Masters by Joseph J. Weed (Feb 1, 1971)

Work of Invisible Helpers by Amber M. Tuttle (1996)

X3, Healing, Entities, and Aliens. Adrian Dvir (2003)

Xing Yi Quan by Sun Lu Tang

Yoga Sutras of Patanjali, The by Patanjali and Charles Johnston

You Forever by T. Lobsang Rampa (Sep 1, 1990)

Your Immortal Reality by Gary R. Renard

NEXT DENSITY™

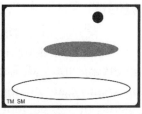

I'll be conducting several efforts through my company *Next Density Research Education and Development Center, LLC.* You may like to be involved in some of these research, education, and development efforts. In these efforts you can learn valuable multidimensional skills.

Next Density™ Out-of-Body / Astral Projection Course I. This is a 2-month practical course on developing out-of-body / astral projection basic skill, led by Darryl E Berry Jr. The course material is *Travel Far.* There will include personal instruction and coaching, group exercises, and group instruction.

Next Density™ Extraterrestrial and Interdimensional Contact Initiative I. This is a new research and development initiative on the practical ability to psychically contact and directly perceive and interact with extraterrestrial/interdimensional beings, led by Darryl E Berry Jr. Building upon my experience and research I'll share techniques to help prepare psychologically for contact, and we'll put these ideas into practice both through personal development at home and through group expeditions out in the field.

For more information and to sign up for these and other efforts visit www.nextdensity.com, or write to Next Density, Darryl E Berry Jr, PO Box 783, Peewee Valley, KY, 40056.

ABOUT THE AUTHOR AND PUBLISHER

My name is **Darryl E Berry Jr**. I'm a long time practitioner, researcher, and observer of all things metaphysical, mystical, and cutting edge, including the out-of-body experience, extraterrestrial life, consciousness development, channeling, telepathy, spirituality especially *A Course in Miracles* and other non-dualistic thought, and fourth-density thought. Through **Next Density™** I'm publishing books by the imprint **Next Density Publishing™**, and building a center called **Next Density Center™** through which to share what I've learned and to establish a nexus of communion, information, development, and progress, to help facilitate the progress of the human race.

My first book, ***Travel Far: A Beginner's Guide to the Out-of-Body Experience, Including First-Hand Accounts and Comprehensive Theory and Methods***, is the first of several books to be published. My next book is entitled *Next Density,* which will outline the general perspective I am presenting, including fourth-density thought, spiritual development, freedom and self-ownership, universal brotherhood, and opening to contact. Volume II of *Travel Far* is in the works as well – the main topic of which is the exploration of planet Mars. There will be a comprehensive book entitled *Exo-Communications* on contacting and interacting with extraterrestrials. There is also a memoir I've penned entitled *My Journey through Gracie Jiu-Jitsu: White to Blue,* on my progress from white to blue belt in the Gracie Jiu-Jitsu system. I can be contacted at www.darryleberryjr.com. Prospective authors interested in having Next Density Publishing™ publish your work can contact me at www.nextdensity.com.

Next Density™

Next Density Center™

Next Density
Publishing™

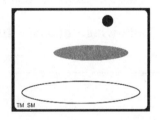

WWW.NEXTDENSITY.COM

WWW.NEXTDENSITYPUB.COM

QUICK ORDER FORM

Email orders: orders@nextdensity.com
Postal orders: Next Density Publishing™, Darryl E Berry Jr, PO Box 783, Peewee Valley, KY, 40056, USA.

Please send me more FREE information on:
__ Other Books
__ Speaking / Seminars
__ Mailing Lists / Newsletters
__ Consulting
__ Research and Development Efforts
__ Courses / Workshops / Retreats

Make checks/money orders payable to Next Density™

Please send the following books, discs, or etcetera:
_____
_____

Name: _____
Company/Organization: _____
Address: _____
City: _____ State: _____ Zip: _____
Telephone: _____
Email: _____

Sales tax: Please add 6% sales & use tax for products shipped to Kentucky, USA addresses.

US Shipping: *Media mail* – Add $3.00 for first book or disc and $1.00 for each additional item. *Air mail* – Add $5.00 for first book or disc and $2.00 for each additional item.
International Shipping: Add $9.00 for first book or disc and $5.00 for each additional item (an estimate – final cost will be emailed prior to shipping).

Next Density™

Next Density Center™

Next Density
Publishing™

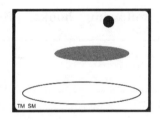

TM SM

WWW.NEXTDENSITY.COM

WWW.NEXTDENSITYPUB.COM

QUICK ORDER FORM

Email orders: orders@nextdensity.com
Postal orders: Next Density Publishing™, Darryl E Berry Jr, PO Box 783, Peewee Valley, KY, 40056, USA.

Please send me more FREE information on:
_ Other Books
_ Speaking / Seminars
_ Mailing Lists / Newsletters
_ Consulting
_ Research and Development Efforts
_ Courses / Workshops / Retreats

Make checks/money orders payable to Next Density™

Please send the following books, discs, or etcetera:
_____
_____

Name: _____
Company/Organization: _____
Address: _____
City: _____ State: _____ Zip: _____
Telephone: _____
Email: _____

Sales tax: Please add 6% sales & use tax for products shipped to Kentucky, USA addresses.

US Shipping: *Media mail* – Add $3.00 for first book or disc and $1.00 for each additional item. *Air mail* – Add $5.00 for first book or disc and $2.00 for each additional item.
International Shipping: Add $9.00 for first book or disc and $5.00 for each additional item (an estimate – final cost will be emailed prior to shipping).